Development Issues

Development Issues

Edited by

P. Vijayalakshmi Reddy

RAWAT PUBLICATIONS

Jaipur • New Delhi • Bangalore • Mumbai • Hyderabad • Guwahati

ISBN 81-316-0250-8

Published by
Prem Rawat for **Rawat Publications**
Satyam Apts, Sector 3, Jawahar Nagar, Jaipur 302 004 (India)
Phone: 0141 265 1748/7006 Fax: 0141 265 1748
E-mail: info@rawatbooks.com
Website: www.rawatbooks.com

New Delhi Office
4858/24, Ansari Road, Daryaganj, New Delhi 110 002
Phone: 011 2326 3290

Also at Bangalore, Mumbai, Hyderabad and Guwahati

Typeset by Rawat Computers, Jaipur
Printed at Chaman Enterprises, New Delhi

Contents

Editor's Note

Development is an ongoing process reflecting change and growth. As a process it is dependent on various institutions of the society which influence the pace and direction of development. Development aims at enhancing the community resources and brings about progress by the participation of the people. It involves reducing the poverty, inequalities, injustice and deprivation of the people. It encompasses the public concerns in developing social policy and economic initiatives to fight poverty, hunger, illiteracy, unemployment, illness and lack of basic infrastructure. The socio-economic and environmental challenges being faced by the present world in terms of growing intolerance, conflict for ownership of natural resources, global warming, population explosion, immense pressure on the existing infrastructure and increasing deprivation has made development a complex phenomenon.

The socio-economic divide between the developed, developing and underdeveloped countries is increasing. The World Bank works to bridge this divide. One of the world's largest sources of development assistance, the World Bank supports the efforts of developing countries' governments to build schools and health centres, provide water and electricity, fight disease, and protect the environment. It is one of the United Nations' specialized agencies, and is made up of 184 member countries. In 2004, the World Bank provided $20.1 billion for 245 projects in developing countries worldwide, with its finance and/or technical expertise aimed at helping these countries reduce poverty.

The national, state and local governments are not only responsible but may also be instrumental to ensure development. The Planning Commission, the state development agencies and the panchayati system needs to work in synchronization for the grass-roots development. Since the Indian economy is largely dependent on agriculture and its associated sectors, and more than 70 per cent of Indian population staying in rural areas, rural development becomes significant whereby government may be the largest contributor. The various community development and poverty alleviation programmes and policies lose their essence owing to lacunae in its implementation. The efforts of the government should not only be directed towards economic development but also social development, reflected by the Human Development Index.

But the government as a system has its limitations since the system can work under certain conditions. In this background, the role of the civil society organizations mainly the non-government organizations (NGOs) and the society itself increases tremendously.

NGOs are voluntary social work organizations that render help to government and society for improvement of quality of life of people. From education to health to environment and to poverty alleviation, the reach of NGOs touches every part of life. NGOs play a vital role in complementing government efforts and help fill in the gaps while systematically orienting the government determination and the group conscience. NGOs work with wide range and categories of people in different regions and areas; the poor and deprived; age and gender-specific groups; occupational groups (e.g., farmers, weavers, fishermen etc.); and persons adversely affected by disease, natural and man-made disasters. The multi-task orientation includes social development by means of working in the areas of sustainable development, health, education, women empowerment, microfinance, biodiversity etc. The humanitarian, non-profit, innovative approach of the NGOs makes them a vital means to ensure development. Even the United Nations recognizes the vital role that civil society organizations play in partnership with governments, UN agencies, and others. A recent example of this type of partnership was reflected in the General Assembly Special Session for Children held at United Nations headquarters in 2002. More then 1,700 NGO representatives from 88 different countries attended the special session.

The most crucial role for development is played by the society itself. Society manifests itself through these agencies. The voice and participation of the people in policy formulation and implementation is the key for development. The values held by the society and the awareness among the people of the society is a significant factor in community development. The papers in the present volume are categorized into four subheads—Development Issues, Natural Resources in Development, Role of Government NGOs and Community in Development, Diversities in Development

V. Janardhan in the paper "The Issue is Earth Itself: Development and Planetary Disaster", addresses the basic problem regarding the sustainability of planet earth, of its ability to sustain future life. The capitalist development has been making for a bankruptcy of the resources of earth that is believed to be non-renewable. This paper explains about the green capitalism and examines the changing sociology of capitalism.

B.C. Muthayya in his paper "Role of Rural Institutions and Banks in Rural Development" examines the changes in the approach and focus of rural development over a period of 10 Five Year plans. The major issues of concern for development in which the rural institutions and banks can play an important role are—technology, environmental management, poverty alleviation, human resource development. Rural development should include decisions on employment generation, infrastructural development, institutional support for sustainable development, human development etc.

In the paper "Reflections on the Strategies for Operationalizing Sustainable Development in Governance: Framework in Developing Countries with Specific Reference to

India", Thilotham R. Kolanu attempts to analyze the strategies for operationalizing sustainable development in the exciting governance framework in India and qualitatively evaluates opportunities and constraints for institutionalizing the tool of strategic environmental assessment both from national and regional perspective. It also presents a way forward for concretely moving in the direction of operationalizing sustainable development.

Vinita Pandey in her paper "Privatization of Water: Impact on Development", questions the feasibility of privatization of most vital natural resource for human survival, i.e., water. Privatization is being sought as a significant solution. In this background, the paper argues that privatization of water is not the solution, rather, alternative by bringing in water reforms and transparent water management policies will ensure that management of water belongs to communities.

In the article "Sustainable Development in Agriculture: Role of Some NGOs in Western Maharashtra", R.B. Patil, deals with some of the NGOs which are working in the area of sustainable development in agriculture. The various activities of NGOs like documentation, research and standardization of organic practices, distribution of water on equal justice, soil and water conservation, tree plantation etc. have been discussed in detail.

In the paper "Natural Resource Management and Development", S. Jeevananda Reddy signifies, two natural resources that are instrumental in development—land and water. The development activities should consolidate itself in sustainability. The development activities sponsored by the government are aimed only at few groups and unfortunately cause environmental destruction and human miseries. The various issues related with HUDA, Himayatsagar and Osmansagar lakes, Shamshabad International Airport, Outer Ring Road in Hyderabad etc., are highlights.

Swarna S. Vepa in her paper "Role Assigned to Women by Development Advocates: Implications to Gender Equity", examines the role played by organizations like government, non-government, international aid agencies, World Bank (which have been combinedly called as Advocates of Development) in shaping up the policies and programmes for rural women in India. Most of the programmes by these organizations have been successful in roping in women belonging to the poverty groups, lower castes and tribal communities. In this background, the paper makes an assessment of how much gender equity or upward mobility has been achieved.

In the paper "Local Governance Institutions and Citizen Leadership: A Means to Promote Participatory Development: A PRIA Experience in Mahbubnagar District of AP", Praveen. Sriramshetty, highlights the socio-economic and political discrimination and oppression of the elite towards the marginalized wherein they are denied to access information and resources. The paper showcases the approach adopted by PRIA to promote participatory development through democratic decentralization. It is thereby emphasized that strong local governance institutions and citizen leadership through participation shall lead to development.

The paper "Dimensions of NGOs Working with Women and Children in Rajasthan" by Jyotsana Rajvanshi is based on the assessment report of the project conducted on networking of organization with women and children in Rajasthan in coordination with UNICEF Rajasthan. The assessment report and resource directory will serve as a valuable source of information to voluntary sector professionals, government departments, corporates, journalists etc.

D.N. Reddy in his paper "NGO Sector in India in the Era of Globalization and Economic Liberalization" describes about the NGO sector which is very vibrant in India and is recognized for its capacity innovativeness and concern for the people. NGO sector is a legitimate legal tool which can bring in unbelievable strength to the people's movements in many ways, by transferring information across the world.

In the article "Role of NGOs in Tribal Development: An Overview", Jadi Musalaiah reviews and analyzes the objectives and the role of NGOs in the area of tribal development. It explains the various schemes and their implementation through various NGOs along with other institutions since independence. It also proposes certain initial inputs for the development of tribals through NGOs.

The paper "Role of NGOs in Empowerment of Women: A Study of Self-Help Groups" by K. Padmavathi reviews the works of the NGOs in alignment with self-help groups in order to assess the empowerment of women, its extent and lacunae if any. The paper attempts to analyze the fast track to women development through SHGs which works on a range of issues such as health, nutrition, agriculture, forestry, social awareness etc. besides income generation activities including micro-credit.

In the paper "Job Loss Problem and Issue of Alternative Livelihood: Case Study of Karimnagar Cooperative Spinning Mills" by M. Bharath Bhushan and E. Revathi, the problem of job loss has been analyzed as both economic and social problem. In the wake of industrial sickness or privatization the problem has become very grave. The issue of job loss as emerging social problem is examined in the context of Andhra Pradesh and a detailed assessment of the complexity is presented with reference to Karimnagar Cooperative Spinning Mills. The paper also examines the pattern of changing livelihoods owing to closure of an enterprise and draws conclusions for strengthening the community effort in understanding and addressing the issue of new social problem.

In the paper "Community Driver Development in Andhra Pradesh", C.P. Nagi Reddy, explains about Andhra Pradesh District Poverty Initiatives Project (APDPIP)—its objectives, components, scope to implementation. It is emphasized that any project/ programme/policy can yield results including development only if 'community' becomes an instrumental factor i.e., to say that the development programmes should not only be community centric but also that community should be an active participant in the development process.

In the paper "Regional Diversities in Indian Development", Sunanda Pande examines the prevalence of diversities in Indian economy which is related to diverse history and diversity in Indian constitution. Development, thus has to consider the diversities prevailing in India. The changes and reforms in Indian economy are thus instrumental in bringing about overall development including that of marginalized groups.

Acknowledgements

I express my deep sense of gratitude to UGC-SERO Hyderabad which has been instrumental in hosting the two-day national seminar on "Development Issues: The Role of World Bank/Banks, Government, NGOs and Society" on 23–24 June, 2006 and bringing about this volume. The Principal, Nizam College, Prof. S. Satyanarayana, was very supportive during all the stages of seminar. I am thankful to Prof. Mohd. Suleman Siddiqi, Vice Chancellor, Osmania University and Prof. Mutha Reddy, Registrar, Osmania University, for their encouragement. I owe my thanks to Department of Sociology, Nizam College, Hyderabad, which has been the driving force for the national seminar.

My deep sense of appreciation to all the participants and delegates from all over the country who participated and kept the discussion very lively throughout the seminar enhancing the intellectual framework. I also appreciate the cooperation of the authors in complying with the corrections and queries that were put forth to them from time to time.

I owe much to the present Vice Chancellor Prof. T. Tirupathi Rao, who encouraged this endeavour. I am also grateful to the Dean, UGC and the UGC Unit, Osmania University for funding the project.

P. Vijayalakshmi Reddy

1 The Issue is Earth Itself

Development and Planetary Disaster

V. Janardhan

The notion of development, in theory and in/as practice, has had widespread acceptance the world over. Indeed, very few ideas have generated such a quantum and extent of *consent* as the notion of development. The ideology of development has surpassed, in terms of acceptability and effectiveness, most other ideologies historically. In fact, most ideologies have also claimed development as one of their basic planks. Development is the magic wand that would supposedly remove deprivation and turn every place into a land of milk and honey. The notion of development is dear as much to a bureaucrat, a technocrat, an entrepreneur and a contractor as it is to a Liberal, a Marxist, a Leninist, a Maoist, and a fascist of all varieties; the homegrown as well as overseas (of course, there are some 'basic' differences). In short, development is, undeniably, an *article of faith*. The most notable dissenters in this regard may perhaps be the Gandhians. But then, their influence over the dominant ideas and models of development have been negligible, to say the least.

Development is inextricably bound up with the idea of *modernity*. Its roots can be traced to the very beginnings of modern western philosophy. It is from this time on that the subject-object dichotomy comes into the organized thought process. Man as the subject and nature as the object that has to be engaged with, worked upon and conquered; nature as the giver of its bounties and man as the taker. Closely linked to this idea is the conviction that man is the most exalted of all the species and that this planet is meant for man. This idea was expounded with utmost clarity by Rene Descartes, considered to be the father of modern western philosophy.

Descartes, in his *Discourse on Method*, operated on two assumptions, one ancient and the other, entirely new. According to Peter Schouls "The ancient assumption is that there is a rational God who has created a world which operates on rational laws or principles, as well as human beings in this world whose nature it is to be rational and free. The new perspective is that rational human beings should be able to *use* this world to make it work for them through the sciences of 'mechanics' (no more sweat in the provision of daily needs), 'medicine' (no more pain and indefinite postponement of death), and 'morals' (no more anxiety resulting from interpersonal and international quarrels)" (2000: 5–6).

Schouls observes that "this new perspective is one which rejects preoccupation with a paradise lost in a distant past or paradise to be regained in a non-earthly future through the grace of God, and which accepts as a challenge the use of human rationality and 'generosity' to create on earth the good life of freedom from labour, illness and anxiety. It is an attitude which makes the world of 'nature' an object of instrumental value (it exists primarily to serve human needs and aspirations), and which firmly plants the idea of infinite progress in the western mind" (ibid.).

The greater man exerted himself, the greater the earth would yield. The ideology of labour, of perseverance ('industry'), of science and the scientific method, of devotion to work and, correspondingly a work ethic were at the core of the development of capitalism. Saint-Simon, a pioneering sociologist, celebrated the development of industrial civilization. To him, mankind had reached the adult stage with the advent of the modern period. Herbert Marcuse observes that, to Saint-Simon "The new era is that of industrialism, which brings with it a guarantee that it can fulfill all human potentialities. Society as a whole is based on industry. Industry is the only guarantor of its existence, and the unique source of all wealth and prosperity. The state of affairs which is most favourable to industry is, therefore, most favourable to society. This is the starting point as well as the goal of all our efforts" (Marcuse, 1941: 330–31).

Marcuse observes that "Saint-Simon began with a predominantly optimistic view of industrial society—the rapid progress of all productive forces, he thought, would soon blot out the growing antagonisms and the revolutionary upheavals within the modern social system. The new industrial order was above all a positive one, representing the affirmation and fruition of all human endeavour for a happy and abundant life." (ibid.). Thus, Saint-Simon became the founder of modern positivism which has been most conducive to the idea of man as subject and nature as object. Further, the progress of the industrial system presupposed that the struggle between classes became transformed into a struggle against nature, in which all the social classes joined (ibid.: 332). Thus, Saint-Simon visualized an eventual societal consensus to emerge, a consensus regarding (industrial) development as bringing about a society of supreme happiness and prosperity.

The above positive reading of society can have one wondering whether Saint-Simon, as well as Auguste Comte, another pioneering social thinker, would have implied, as many do today explicitly, the 'end of history', the 'end of ideology' and so forth, a couple of centuries back itself!

Meanwhile, even Marx's position lent itself favourably to the idea of what later came to be considered as development. In his introduction to Marx's *Contribution to the Critique of Political Economy*, Maurice Dobb observes that, "whereas for Hegel the dialectic as a principle and structural pattern of development started from abstract being as mind or spirit, for Marx the dialectic of development started from nature, and from man as an integral part of nature. But while part of nature and subject to the determinism of its laws, man as a conscious being was at the same time capable of struggling with and against nature of subordinating it and ultimately transforming it for his own purposes. This he did by consciously devised productive and creative activity. This human activity that differentiated man from nature and from most animate creatures was productive labour. Human history accordingly began from this dialectic of man's struggle with nature, and essentially consisted in the various forms and stages assumed by productive labour in its development and progress" (Dobb in Marx, 1970: 7).

However, as the *dialectic* unfolded, it was becoming clearer that, capitalism even while making nature an object of exploitation, had made living and dead labour also as objects of 'exploitation'. Radical critiques and ideologies such as Marxism and anarchism now articulated *riposte* measures, made prognoses and desired a transcendence of capitalism. But then the argument was for the 'meek inheriting the earth', if it may be put that way. It was for ending the exploitation of man by man but not exploitation of the earth by man. Quite inevitably, at this stage, a Robert Thomas Malthus could be made to look like a clown.

At this stage, what was opposed was not 'accumulation' but the distribution of the social cake. The main contention was *how* it ought to be distributed. This question could be most favourably answered depending on what sort of society and social structure would be brought into existence. Hardly any 'organic' intellectual of the time then thought of the earth question. It was either the 'human' question or more specifically to some, the 'class' question. The earth was taken for granted; it was a given. Not to exploit it was a sin.

It thus came to pass that both the world views, ideologies and practises of capitalism and socialism came to rest solidly on the base of *industrialism*. On this aspect, a Saint-Simon, a Marx, a Lenin, etc., can be observed to be in full accord. As mentioned earlier, Saint-Simon had observed that what was good for industry was good for society. The Marxists would have only added the word 'socialist' in parenthesis. Thus, the model of development whose chief features were rapid industrialization, increased use of sophisticated energy-demanding technology, urbanization, etc., originating *organically* in the early starting nations, became, deliberately, a societal and cultural *choice* in post-colonial societies. The state became a developmental state, a welfare state, a state that worked for economic growth with social justice. It stood for the last man assuring that everyone would have a place under the sun. Even our home-grown 'Marxist-Leninist' intellectuals read positive signals in the state though reserving their ambivalence for appropriate occasions!; such as when deliberating in learned circles, on its 'class' character. They were also instrumental in spawning a new school of thought called 'development planning'. Today, it is no longer the privilege of that esoteric section of society called the economists. Any roadside NGO promoter can call himself a development expert. In a way, his own development if not survival is assured depending on which corporate-originated foundation sponsors him and from which part of the world. The NGO person is the latest to qualify as a mercenary.

Today, the role of the state in development has been undergoing a redefinition. It is not required for the state to participate directly in the development process anymore. What is now required of it is to act as a *facilitator*. The state has to basically provide for the infrastructure—roads, communications, etc., and leave the rest to private capital and international agencies who know what is best for them. The state is also expected to remove 'roadblocks' to foreign investment in almost all sectors of industry, commerce and services. Not to do so would send the wrong signals to global investors and would be against the spirit of globalization and liberalization. Saint-Simon advocated in his time that what is good for industry is good for society. The protagonists of industry and development say much the same today. The process of globalization has only accentuated this advocacy much further. This is the background to the problem being posed in this paper.

The Problem

The basic problem addressed in the present paper is regarding the sustainability of planet earth, of its ability to sustain future life. More than two centuries of capitalist development has been making for a bankruptcy of the resources of the earth that is believed to be largely non-renewable, at least in the short and medium run. Planned development efforts are also following the same models and principles. Historically, capitalism meant production of commodities whose main characteristics are exchange-value, exploitation of labour and more and more accumulation of capital. 'Development' also stands mostly for this type of value-creation predicated on the exploitation of the earth's resources apart from generating a phenomenal quantum of waste. Today, a situation is being reached where "humanity's production and waste consumption exceed the earth's capacity to create new resources and absorb waste. Natural capital is being exploited at high rates to support current resource use reducing the earth's ability to support future life" (Sagar Dhara, 2006).

There have been several empirical studies and theoretical texts that have highlighted the problem. Apart from certain tendencies within Marxism, the critiques have also emanated from Gandhian thought, by think tanks such as the World Watch Institute, Club of Rome, etc., and individuals such as E.F. Schumacher. But the problem has been much more complex. Meanwhile, humans have been eroding their natural capital. According to ecological studies, the *ecological footprint* of human society started exceeding the earth's biocapacity by around mid-seventies in the last century. Today, nearly 1.4 times the earth's biocapacity is needed to sustain the current level of human activity. "Ecological footprint is a measure of the amount of nature's biocapacity required annually to sustain a population. By comparing a population's footprint with its biocapacity, ecological footprint analysis suggests whether the population is living within its ecological means" (ibid.).

What is to be done? ... And by whom?

The present dominant models of development do not effectively question the degradation of the earth including the catastrophic levels of pollution being experienced today. Development policies and practises only tend to draw more and more people into the ambit of the capitalist world. People become, on one hand, the global labour power working for capital as well as, on the other, the consumers of products made by capitalist industry. Mindless production and consumption is precisely what is causing the problem. It can be observed that the present development paradigm only exists to create more and more markets for the products of global capital.

The present paper does not pin its faith in any great revolution or other upheaval that would sweep away the undesirable order and bring in a new order, a new set of institutions, etc. Rather, it believes in engaging the present, with the present, with the *existing* institutions both inside and outside of them. This necessarily means states, and now increasingly, the 'international state', non-state regional, national and international actors, etc. While these have various degrees of proximity and linkage to the corporate capitalist world, it is the latter which has to be essentially and ultimately addressed. From a very practical standpoint, it is only the corporate companies the world over, particularly the top global 50 companies, banks and financial institutions having a global sweep, that can initiate the process of the long haul of renewal. It is only they who have the power, the resources and the managerial skills to put into operation effective measures. Part of the effort would be to make them look inwards, at themselves and at their business strategies and goals and see where these are landing all of us. Fundamentally, they have to look at their production systems including raw material consumption, energy, conversion processes, toxicity, waste generation, etc., and self-imposed stringent norms and best practises. Mass production has to be replaced by flexible production (to some extent this has already started). For starters, a march towards a *green capitalism* has to be commenced. The present paper will explain subsequently, the grounds of possibilities for making these things happen *the changing sociology of capitalism* that has seen greater popular participation in contemporary capitalism. Hitherto it was said "we are all socialists now". Today, it is "we are all capitalists now". For example, most of us are investors in one way or another; even the most innocuous insurance policyholder whose premiums can be invested in the corporate sector, mutual funds being another example. This tendency is on the rise given the expansion of modern economic and financial institutions, the attenuation of distance between town and countryside and the rise of rural and semi-rural entrepreneurship particularly of women. Many women's groups are having direct contractual relationships with the corporate world and are part of the latter's distribution mechanism.

Another associated feature is the growth of agribusiness. Companies are perfecting their supply chain by entering into institutional arrangements with the peasantry such as contract farming; ITC and Pepsi being prime examples. This is but one dimension of the move by the corporate sector to penetrate the rural hinterland which is going to be the market of the near future. Companies like ITC Bhadrachalam have grasped the importance of renewable natural resources, both as raw material and as an ecological issue. Raising the level of ecological awareness among companies in general could very well become a matter for advocacy. At least in the spirit of enlightened self-interest, companies would understand the ecological argument.

There is also being witnessed a new development in corporate advertising and marketing. Lucy Aitken (*The Economic Times*, 6 September, 2006) reports that "a growing body of evidence suggests that there is a tangible business benefit to be gained by 'greenifying' advertising but only if it is a genuine message and not 'green-wash'". The latter accusation would be made against companies that preach but do not practise. For instance, Aitken says, BP and Shell spend colossal money on green advertising but critics point out that these companies do not even spend less than two per cent of their annual investment each year on renewable energy resources.

Aitken further reports that a 2005 Ethical Consumerism Report, conducted by the Co-op Bank, NEF and the Futures Foundation, revealed that 57 per cent of consumers had recommended a company on the basis of its responsible reputation. Consumers spent 25.8 billion pounds on ethical goods and services in 2004, an increase of 15 per cent on 2003, a sign of encouragement. Aitken (ibid.) observes that "consumers are seeing for themselves the effects of climate change. Droughts, rising fuel prices and more media coverage of green issues have all served as triggers for people to reassess their behaviour. Now they will think twice before automatically filling up the petrol tank or having a long, hot soak in the bath instead of a quick shower. If individuals are taking responsibility for their own actions, it is no surprise that they want to seek out companies and brands that are making an effort to do the same".

How should companies respond to this growing section of consumers? Aitken has several suggestions. Firstly, "doom and gloom get you nowhere ... . The emphasis must be on the financial gain synonymous with being more carbon-aware, particularly for smaller organizations. And regardless of whether an advertisement targets business or consumers, the fear factor should always make way for optimism. Most importantly, any advertiser considering going green needs to protect itself against its critics by embracing sustainability internally too ... . A new value system is required which ultimately recognizes that the ultimate end is where the value lies; namely, a sustainable future for business and the planet".

Secondly, the *internal world of capitalism* is also changing, the world over. Many decades ago itself, sociologists such as Ralf Dahrendorf observed the changes in capitalism since Marx's lifetime. An important change, according to Dahrendorf, was the separation of ownership from control. This eventually became the managerial revolution whose foremost commentator has been James Burnham (1941). Control became concentrated in the hands of managerial strata while ownership became more diffused. While access to this strata professionally became a matter of education and hard work, one can argue that the *democratization* of companies began with this development. Growth of shareholder and institutional capitalism pushed this process further. Managerial excesses have sought to be addressed by putting various control and accountability mechanisms in place. Prime examples are the theory and practice of corporate governance and corporate social responsibility. The idea of corporate governance particularly gives primacy to the concept of the stakeholder. The latter enunciates that shareholders are not the only people to whom the company and its management have to be accountable. There are other stakeholders too including the community and the environment in which the company concerned has its operations.

The point is that the stakeholders external to the company such as the community/neighbourhood have to be active in the new order. Presently, the activism that one finds in this respect is focused on saying 'No' to industry in the concerned area. This practise has to change. The new regime (with its appropriate array of institutions) must be one that processes the conflict that arises between industry and its socio-physical context, and brings about a well-negotiated agreement among the stakeholders. Imminent in this agreement *or even a contract* are the various manners of making the company accountable to society and environment/ecology of the region, agreement on standards for various purposes ranging from usage of natural resources to pollution, etc. In this context, the new laws such as the Right to Information Act assume relevance and contribute to the making of an open society.

It is contended in this paper that a vision of the sort envisaged above is indeed possible. The institutions that can bring this about are precisely those that have been listed out in the subtitle of the present seminar, each contributing in their own way. They include banks and financial institutions, NGOs, CBOs, besides the state institutions from Panchayat to parliament. It is only when all these bodies act in concert that the future would be bright for planet earth.

References

Aitken, Lucy (2006), "For Greener Pastures" in *The Economic Times*, September 6.

Burnham, James (1941), *The Managerial Revolution*, New York, Doubleday.

Dahrendorf, Ralf (1959), *Class and Class Conflict in an Industrial Society*, London, Routledge.

Dhara, Sagar (2006), *Working Notes*, Hyderabad, Cerana Foundation, (unpublished).

Dobb, Maurice in Karl Marx (1970), *A Contribution to the Critique of Political Economy*, Moscow, Progress.

Marcuse, Herbert (1941), *Reason and Revolution: Hegel and the Rise of Social Theory*, London, Routledge and Kegan Paul.

Schouls, Peter (2000), *Descartes and the Possibility of Science*, Ithaca, Cornell.

2 Role of Rural Institutions and Banks in Rural Development

B.C. Muthayya

Rural development has made changes in its approach and focus over a period of ten Five-Year plans. Varieties of objectives constituted our Five-Year plans depending upon the concern of the time. For example, development of rural economy, improving agricultural production, reducing disparities, development with social justice, poverty alleviation, employment generation, human development and so on, ultimately aiming to usher in self-reliance. The approaches also made changes from area development, target group to integrated rural development. Currently, the main focus is on poverty eradication, improving agricultural production, employment generation—either asset-based, skill-based or wage based employment and also to improve the quality of life of rural people in terms of provisions of health, nutrition, education, drinking water, roads and housing. However, the expectations as enunciated in the policies fell short of achievements for varied reasons though money was not a constraint after the Sixth Plan. In between the country had to cope with natural catastrophes like drought, floods, earthquake, cyclone, tsunami apart from man-made disasters and manage its ill effects with relief and rehabilitation of affected people. This kind of happenings slow down the process of development efforts, one of the contributing factors for success or failure of our development efforts could be the way institutions, meant for implementation of the variety of programmes, functioned in a given context.

In the process of rural development, it was envisaged particularly after late seventies and early eighties to work out partnerships with banks, NGOs and other international agencies to augment the process of development. In poverty alleviation programmes the banks have a crucial role to play by providing a major chunk of the project cost with subsidy being contributed by the government. The NGOs were expected to serve as link-pins between the government agencies, banks and people through mobilizing the people, creating awareness of the policies, programmes and procedures and provide post-scheme loan support and guidance. They were supposed to play the role of catalyst or facilitator of the development process. Banks were supposed to provide the financial input as envisaged and participate in this endeavour along with other agencies of the government. Though all the agencies created by the government like DRDA, DIC, KVIB, KVIC, Panchayat Raj bodies were aware of their respective roles in augmenting the process of development, and heeded but, this did not result in commensurate measures as per expectations. The banks and NGOs are also aware of their roles as there were plenty of guidelines for this purpose both issued by the government and the apex banks periodically but could not yield results. Even today people are discussing how the banks should be involved and motivated to participate in the development process and what could be the factors hindering their active involvement in this endeavour.

The government agencies feel that unless the banks participate effectively by making loans available on time, it is difficult to achieve results. Therefore, it is not a question of not being aware of the respective roles each of these institutions have to play or warrants any fresh guidelines about the roles they have to play in context of implementation of rural development programmes.

The problem is ineffective role performance as a consequence lack of motivation and attitudinal changes among the incumbents of these institutions. There is more of role confusion as each one expects the other to first what is expected of his organization. Coordination within the government institutions and sectoral departments and also with other participating institutions has been a perennial problem. The misfortune is everyone seems to be interested in rural development but it is difficult to see a worthwhile effort in implementing a given programme in letter and spirit. A effective programme implementation requires a cooperative and coordinated effort between the government agencies, banks and NGOs in creating awareness about the programmes, benefits provided, procedure for availing it, helping identification of schemes relevant to a given area and matching the schemes with the felt needs of the targeted people, help in grounding the scheme and take follow-up action and help in marketing the produce to get a reasonable price. If this coordinated effort could be managed, the exploitative role of the moneylenders, traders could be eliminated. The exploitation by middlemen, moneylenders and traders has led the farmers to a large extent to commit suicides. The question is if all the multiple agencies which are interdependent had worked unitedly by effectively converging their services at the delivery level, whether most of the suicides could have been prevented. Therefore, role identification is a futile exercise unless the role incumbents are thorough about their role expectations and methods of converting them into action. This calls for a change in their outlook among all those involved in the process of development in terms of their values, attitudes, motivations and concern for the poor. It requires dynamism in role performance rather than a static approach. If the policies and programmes are dynamic, it requires a dynamic personnel in these organizations to convert the policies into action.

If these are the organizations created for the purpose of rural development, then let us now have a look at the major issues of concern for development at large and expect these organizations to help in resolving these issues.

Methods to Accelerate the Process of Development

In the context of globalization, one has to move faster in all our productive endeavours and improve upon the quality of our products to meet the world standards to be recognized as a competitor and to find markets for our products. Adoption of modern technology and technological innovations can facilitate the process of faster development. New technologies will lead to healthier lives, greater social freedom, increased knowledge and more productive livelihood. Technology is a tool and not a just a reward for growth and development. Technology is created in response to market pressures not the needs of the people who have little purchasing power. Technology has a multiplier effect creating a vicious circle, increasing people's knowledge, health and productivity, raising income and building capacity for future invention, all leading to human development. Education and skills are required to use technology effectively. Rapid growth is the main instrument for poverty alleviation.

Environmental Management

People and environment have a close affinity, as one supports the other. However, over a period of time, exploitation of the natural resources beyond a limit has affected both the environment and the people. In India, the forest cover is expected to be 33 per cent of the total geographical area but now it is below 20 per cent with wide variations across the states. The afforestation programmes have been taken up with peoples' participation making little progress.

Emphasis on Poverty Alleviation

The right to be free of the crushing burden of poverty must be counted among the most fundamental of human rights. Poverty is embedded in all realms of existence of the poor people and extends beyond income. As per the official statistics (1999–2000), 27 per cent of the people are below the poverty line. These percentages keep varying from time to time and from one state to another.

Though a variety of special programmes have been implemented for the identified target groups, the results are far from satisfactory. The percentage of people below the poverty line seem to be bulging as years roll by.

Human Resource Development

During the late seventies, India showed concern for HRD including women's development and their empowerment along with the weaker sections of the society. India's rural literacy is 59 per cent and women literacy in the rural areas is 47 per cent. In the context of globalization, in order to make people capable of becoming active participants in the productive process absorbing new technological innovations, it is essential to have minimum education coupled with the needed knowledge and skills as these have a premium in the developmental process, particularly with the onset of information technology. Our educational system needs to gear up to this gigantic task of spreading literacy and augmenting the learning process by identifying, processing and disseminating the required information and skills to the people to create the knowledge base to facilitate the developmental process. Health, nutrition and family welfare are the other areas of concern for HRD as it provides the physical base to meet the competition around the world.

Based on these larger issues, the current rural development should encompass decisions on the following issues:

Employment Generation

What kind of employment should be provided to those in need—whether it is asset-based (gainful), wage-based, or skill-based or an effective combination of these for effective sustenance at a particular level of employment as experience has it that each one by itself may not guarantee movement of the people above the poverty line. It may be worthwhile to consider a combination of wage and gainful employment for those above 40 years and wage and skill-based employment for those below 40 years, more particularly for the unemployed rural youth. Now the National

Employment Guarantee Scheme is being implemented to provide some solace temporarily to those who are unemployed.

Infrastructural Development

Programme support in terms of facilities and services like for inputs (in agriculture and industry), finance (effective credit system), marketing are a perquisite for achieving the expected goals. The President's initiative in regard to providing urban amenities in rural areas (PURA) holds promise well for the future.

Providing for social consumption needs such as health care, nutrition support, education, safe drinking water, housing and family welfare. This need not be overemphasized as in rural areas, all these are still wanting much more than what could be provided over the previous Five-Year Plan periods.

Institutional Support for Sustainable Development

To what extent the government and its variety of agencies, Panchayat Raj institutions, NGOs can provide the needed support in not only identifying the problem areas, removing the bottlenecks and implementing the programmes as per the policy guidelines for the benefit of those for whom they are intended. As of now, there seems to be quite an amount of overlap in the functioning of these organizations and hence a convergence of these institutional arrangements at the grass-roots level is a requirement for effective programme management to achieve the desired results. Along with democratic decentralization, administrative decentralization is a prerequisite as people at the grass-roots level are better judges of what needs to be done and how it has to be done.

Apart from this, these institutions should provide the social support to the targeted groups which means verbal and non-verbal communication that reduces people's uncertainty about themselves, the situation or their relationships with the support providers and thus enhances their sense of control over their destinies.

Human Development

The major focus of rural development from the context of globalization should be human development. The focus of the eighth Five-Year Plan was on human development. People are the crucial but most unpredictable variable of development among all other variables influencing its process. The effort should be to develop the human capital facilities to acquire knowledge and skills through education and training coupled with information technology to act in new ways, and social capital socially structured relationships between individuals and groups to achieve individual and community goals supported by knowledge and responsibility-based empowerment. People often seem to be apathetic or powerless because of temporary lack of awareness, confidence and competence to take action to effect change. Poor people are characterized by a thwarting of need gratification and yearning for self-expression, a feeling of abasement, a morbid dependence on others, lack of confidence and trust in their inner resources, jealousy and hatred against the real and perceived others (officials or leaders), for their plight. The ecology of poverty is conducive to lack of stimuli essential for proper human development. Self-defeating behaviour usually stems from people unable to identify alternate ways of behaviour. Development is fundamentally a learning task. People at the community level need to acquire new skills required for development, not just to receive new information. The ultimate aim of human development is to develop people's competence (knowledge and skills) and commitment (confidence and motivation) and positive attitudes to change. The purpose of information giving process should be to convince them about the need for change, effect the change, get them to commit to the change and finally to convert them to new ways of thinking, feeling and doing oriented to further development.

3 Reflections on the Strategies for Operationalizing Sustainable Development in Governance

Framework in Developing Countries with Specific Reference to India

Thilotham R. Kolanu

Operationalizing sustainable development as a concept is one of the major challenges faced by state as well as non-state actors involved in economic growth as well as developmental processes. Since the Rio Earth Summit in 1992, the international community, national and local governments, private sector organizations, NGOs, and others have strived to find ways to operationalize it (UNDP, 2004). While the notion of sustainable development has exhibited broad political appeal but has proven difficult to define in precise terms (Parris and Kates, 2003). Achieving sustainable development will require deep structural changes and new ways of working in all areas of economic, social and political life. This will include promoting pro-poor economic growth and reforming fiscal policies, which negatively affect the poor or promote environmental damage. Analysts have been identifying opportunities that ensure economic practises and lifestyles, sustainable (Lester, 2006). In different sectoral activities and regions, successful initiatives towards triple bottomline are showcased for replication. But experience demonstrates that these 'bottom up' opportunities have often remained 'islands of excellence' and in the realm of possibilities for replication mainly because of the limitations of the macroeconomic policies and institutional mechanisms. For replicating the sustainable approaches across regions and sectors there is a need to correct systemic flaws in 'top down' development as a complement to 'bottom up' development (Auty, 2003). This paper attempts to analyze the strategies for operationalizing sustainable development in the existing governance framework in India as a means to correct 'top down' developments and qualitatively evaluate opportunities and constraints for institutionalizing sustainable development using Strategic Environmental Assessment (SEA) as a tool. It also presents a plausible way forward for concretely moving in the direction of operationalizing sustainable development strategy in India.

Sustainable development as a concept has elements of vagueness with regard to its understanding as well as operationalizing in divergent spatio-temporal contexts. In spite of this vagueness, given the wide appreciation of its underlying philosophy efforts have being made across the world to relook at the systems, processes and culture in business operations and public governance so as to translate sustainable development into current spheres of activities. In the context of business units, attempts to translate sustainable development have led to evolution of tools such as Environmental Management Systems (e.g., ISO 14,001 certificate), Environmental Impact Assessment (EIA), environmental accounting, risk assessment etc., for internalizing environmental externalities. Similarly, for addressing the social, economic and equity concerns in a voluntary proactive manner by business units and means to evaluate their performance tools such as Corporate Social Responsibility (e.g., GRI Guidelines for CSR), Social Compact, Social Accountability (SA 8,000), Equator Principles for Financial Institutions etc., have evolved. Though majority in the corporate world across the globe are yet to give strategic attention to environmental, social, economic and equity dimensions in the regions as well as domains of their operations but there is a wide variety of examples of exemplary work in this context, both in the developed and developing countries.

As it evolved sustainable development is perceived as an inter-generational issue, hence, solutions require strategic choices for the longer time and the capacity to maintain commitments over time, as well as capacities to provide decision makers with adequate information and knowledge to support their decisions (OECD, 2002). With reference to developmental processes and existing governance framework in most of the countries across the world, operationalizing sustainable development concept has been a greater challenge primarily due to the sheer magnitude and diversity in sectoral and regional set-ups and the variety as well as number of entities and individuals involved. Thus, it creates a new institutional difficulty because it not only challenges the government capacities to act rapidly but also it contradicts the way policies and programmes are traditionally formulated and developed (OECD, 2002).

While broad contours of initiatives towards sustainable development across sectors and regions have been initially evolved globally in the form of Agenda 21 at Earth Summit in 1992 but the same were subsequently elaborated in various international conferences and finally culminating in evolution of Plan of Implementation under World Summit on Sustainable Development (WSSD), Millennium Developmental Goals (MDGs). Plan of implementation and MDGs spell out targeted action initiatives and goals for states and their supporting agencies including non-governmental organizations (NGOs). National strategies for sustainable development (NSSDs) are being prepared by various national governments for achieving sustainable development. According to OECD, depending on circumstances, a sustainable development strategy may be viewed as a system comprising the following components:

- Regular multi-stakeholder fora and means for negotiation at national and decentralized levels, with links between them.

- A shared vision and set of broad strategic objectives.
- A set of mechanisms to pursue those objectives in ways that can adapt to change (notably an information system; communication capabilities; analytical processes; international engagement; and co-ordinated means for policy integration, budgeting, monitoring, and accountability).
- Principles and standards to be adopted by sectors and stakeholders, through legislation, voluntary action, market-based instruments, etc.
- Pilot activities, to generate learning and ownership.
- A secretariat or other facility with authority for co-ordinating these mechanisms.
- A mandate for all the above from a high-level, central authority such as the prime minister's office and, to the extent possible, from citizens and business organizations (OECD, 2001).

While the technical, scientific dimension is perhaps more obvious, it is clear that the institutional arrangements which currently exist in many countries, are often not consistent with effective assessment of indirect and cumulative impacts, as well as impact interactions. In practice, the application of these techniques for the identification and assessment of impacts is either limited or has not been developed to its full potential. In developing countries' context, the principal obstacle to environmentally sustainable policies is that of government failure to promote economic and environmental policies that have clearly established benefits (Auty, 2003). Addressing economic, social and environmental concerns simultaneously requires a change in the governance framework that impacts livelihoods and environmental resource use. State interventions and markets must be made to work for the poor and the environment while contributing towards economic growth. Analysts have shown that priority of policy and institutional attention demands of economic growth receive far greater attention than social and equity considerations of the decision makers, similarly social and equity considerations receive higher attention than environmental resource use and conservation dimensions. Hence, an evaluation of the sustainable development strategy by focusing on environmental management concerns clearly demonstrates the preparedness of policies and institutions of a country or region. In the following section an attempt has been made to understand the environmental regime in India and evaluate it against requirements of sustainable development criteria.

Environmental Governance Framework in India

Transparency, accountability, equity, participation and building a sense of belonging and ownership to policies and programmes of the state have a predominant influence on the quality of governance. Thus, the strengths and weaknesses in terms of these qualities should also be taken into account in order to assess the environmental governance of a given region. Environmental governance means—legal instruments to prevent control and/or mitigate environmental damage resulting from production and consumption activities of human beings including enforceable laws and norms that prevent actions that cause environmental damage or require actions that improve the environment; economic instruments such as taxes, charges and levies; subsidies or incentives that induce methods to protect environment and its resources; institutions that interact to improve or maintain environmental quality as desired by policy as well as individuals who man these institutions.

In the process of achieving rapid economic growth, India had to face large number of environmental problems. Environmental governance in India has evolved considerably in the last three decades with increased regulations that have wider dimensions and more power. Gradually, regulatory and institutional mechanisms are incorporated for addressing environmental concerns. Since 1974 to this day large number of regulations have been promulgated to deal with various dimensions of environment in terms of media as well as areas. The two main pollution control statutes in India are the Water (Prevention and Control of Pollution) Act of 1974, and the Air (Prevention and Control of Pollution) Act, which came into being in 1981. Thereafter, parliament passed the Environment (Protection) Act in 1986. This was designed to act as an umbrella legislation for the environment, with responsibility for administering the new legislation falling on the central and state boards. As defined in the EP Act 1986, 'environment' includes not only the natural environment and but also some human effects such as health and material assets. It also requires an analysis of a plan's secondary, cumulative and synergistic effects. The law prohibits the pollution of water bodies and requires that generators of effluents/discharges get the prior consent of the SPCBs. This consent to operate must be renewed periodically. An important initiative in this regard has been introduction of a notification of Environmental Impact Assessment (1994) as part of Environmental Protection Act, 1986. This has promulgated in addressing environmental concerns on project-to-project basis, whereby all new environmentally sensitive investments are mandatorily required to undertake multi-stage environmental clearance.

The Central Pollution Control Board (CPCB) serves as the national board, with oversight powers over the various State Pollution Control Boards (SPCBs) at state level and Pollution Control Committees (PCCs) at union territories (See Figure 1 for an outline of the institutional framework for environmental management in India). CPCB was legislated into existence in 1977, following the implementation of the Water Act. The mandate of the CPCB is to set environmental standards for all plants in India, lay down ambient standards, and coordinate the activities of the SPCBs. SPCBs have the legal authority to conduct periodic inspections of plants to check whether they have the appropriate consent to operate, whether they have effluent treatment plants, take samples for analysis, etc. Some of these inspections are also programmed in response to public requests and litigation. The penalty for non-compliance is fines and imprisonment, but until 1988 the enforcement authority of the SPCBs was very weak. It was limited to criminal prosecution (with its attendant delays) and seeking injunctions to restrain polluters. Now, however, SPCBs have the power to close non-compliant factories or cut-off their water and electricity by administrative orders. The *potential* cost to the plants of non-compliance is thus not trivial, so there should be an incentive for plants to comply with the law. However, compliance depends on *both* monitoring and enforcement of the law by the SPCBs. The functions of SPCBs are as follows:

- Assessment of ambient air quality.
- Assessment of water quality.
- Plan a comprehensive programme for the prevention, control or abatement of water/air pollution.
- Advise the state government on any matter concerning the prevention, control or abatement of water and air pollution and location of industries.
- To organize mass education programmes related to prevention, control or abatement of water/air pollution.
- To inspect any pollution control equipment, industrial plant, manufacturing process and to give direction to such persons involved in prevention, control or abatement of water/air pollution.
- To provide consent to establish or operate an industrial unit under Water Act 1974 and Air Act 1981.
- Assessment of water cess under Water (Prevention and Control) Cess Act, 1977 and to collect the water cess from industries/local bodies/Jal Sansthans etc., and send the same to MOEF every month.
- Identification and assessment of industrial and municipal pollution control sources and control thereof.
- Conducting mass awareness programmes.
- Notification of effluent and emission standards.
- Development of pollution control technologies.
- Instituting legal action against defaulters.
- Issue of authorization under the Hazardous Waste (Management and Handling) Rules, 1989.
- Implementation of Biomedical Waste (Management and Handling) Rules, 1998.
- Implementation of Municipal Solid Waste (Management and Handling) Rules, 2002.
- Implementation of Battery Rules.

Some of SPCBs have increased the institutional capabilities so as to enhance effectiveness of environmental monitoring and compliance. Due credit should also be given to other stakeholders such as NGOs, Media and Judiciary for the progress achieved. Owing to the institutionalized experience of SPCB by and large they have been successful in addressing industrial air and water pollution concerns especially those arising from large industries. Here again the behavioural change in regulated industries is more due to the reputational risks that entail negative publicity due to environmental emissions beyond stipulated norms. Despite a strong legal framework and the existence of a large bureaucracy for dealing with environmental regulation, the public perception is that

Figure 1

Institutional Framework for Environmental Management in India

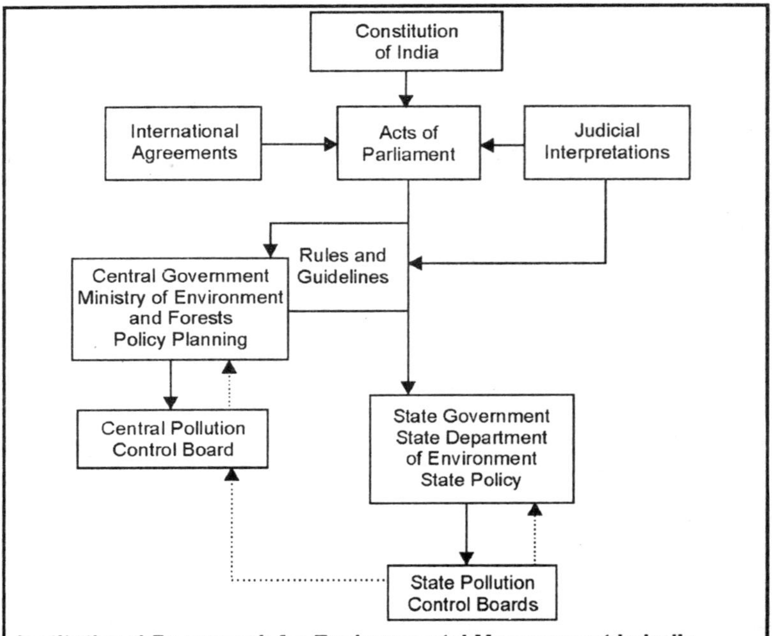

Institutional Framework for Environmental Management in India

Note: —— Indicates flow of authority

······ Indicates reporting mechanism

implementation remains weak. Even the practice of Environmental Impact Assessment (EIA) in India is laden with limitations, as a result experience shows that the effectiveness of this tool in addressing the issues is limited. The primary form of attention towards environment focuses on industrial emissions and the use of command and control instruments of various forms. These involve the setting of standards, monitoring and enforcement that result in only limited compliance due to weak enforcement. For household waste water, soil erosion and other non-industrial environmental problems there is little or no abatement of damage in India as in many other developing countries. While there are positive changes that are achieved in environmental compliance and enforcement there is enormous scope for improving environmental quality with the appropriate changes in the policy and institutional frameworks for environmental management in India.

In the last 30 years of Indian environmental regulatory history, the level of attention paid to monitoring and enforcement has been limited across the country. This in turn has a telling effect both on environmental quality as well as social welfare (Cohen, 1998). One needs to acknowledge the fact that over the years the regulatory regime is becoming stricter and complex but noncompliance to regulatory norms is evident. Governments and society in general cannot afford unlimited resources for environmental monitoring and enforcement to ensure regulatory compliance. Hence, cost dimension of monitoring and enforcement in evolving policies and programmes of SPCBs are essential. As McKean (1980) points out, high enforcement costs and imperfect compliance make regulations less effective than desired. Thus, monitoring and enforcement concerns "should influence choices about how to regulate, and in some instances, about whether to regulate at all" (McKean, 1980).

Recent global evaluation of environmental sustainability of different countries illustrates that India ranked 101 among a 146 countries' study. Thus, it falls into a category of low system score, moderate stress and vulnerability, low capacity and stewardship (Esty et al., 2005). It is due to limitation at the policy level, institutional structural level, programme conceptualization and implementation level that is fraught with limitations which are responsible for this magnitude of environmental costs. Some of the limitations of environmental management practises in the country can be summarized as following:

- Limited attention to environment in the existing policy framework both at the central and state level.
- Limited attention to non-industrial environmental risks in the regulatory regime more so in implementing the existing regulatory norms and standards.
- Regional variations and carrying capacity are not factored in regulatory framework which is more or less uniform for an ecologically diverse country like India.
- Lack of decentralization: Most of the regulations are central government driven and there is limited initiative on part of the state government and implementation is mostly the responsibility of the state pollution control boards working under state government but here also the powers are confined to head offices. As a result, environmental governance in India is highly centralized.
- No stakeholder involvement in evolution of law except for representatives of industry and NGOs are being consulted in a limited manner by coopting them into the expert committees before issuing the new environmental notifications and changing the existing ones.
- Limited spatial as well as sectoral environmental planning experience within the country.
- Limited capacity building initiative that undertakes training need requirements and builds capacities of stakeholders including policy makers and regulators as per the training plan.
- Limited transparency and accountability in environmental governance as most of the people at large are neither informed adequately nor consulted during the decision-making process.

In the last ten years, state and central governments are trying to have an overview of the environmental profile of various regions by bringing out State of Environment (SoE) Reports. This SoE report preparation got formalized in the form of a nationwide initiative by Ministry of Environment and Forests (MoEF), Government of India in 2002 wherein each state is preparing a SoE, which can form the basis for preparation of SEA in the selected state as it provides the required information base for SEA. For the SoE initiative of the MoEF, SEA could be a logical extension whereby policy makers could get the required outputs for initiating environmentally positive change. Also the Draft National Environment Policy 2004 took into concern environmental factors in all development activities proposed to mainstream environmental concerns. The NEP, which was finalized in 2006 recognizes that maintaining a healthy environment is not the state's responsibility alone but also that of every citizen. It states that spirit of partnership should be realized throughout the spectrum of environmental management in the country.

Assessment of Salient Features of National Environment Policy, 2006

Policy recognizes that maintaining a healthy environment is not the state's responsibility alone, but also that of every citizen. It states that spirit of partnership should be realized throughout the spectrum of environmental management. While the state must galvanize its efforts, there should also be recognition by each individual—natural or institutional, of its responsibility towards maintaining and enhancing the quality of the environment. The policy also seeks to stimulate partnerships of different stakeholders, i.e., public agencies, local communities, academic and scientific institutions, the investment community, and international development partners, in harnessing their respective resources and strengths for environmental management. Integration of environmental concerns in all relevant development processes is among the objectives of this policy. It states that inclusion of environmental considerations in sectoral policy making has also been recognized as among the principles underpinning the policy. In order to operationalize these, a mechanism for ensuring necessary due diligence at all levels of government, is proposed to be institutionalized.

Table 1

Assessment of Objectives of National Environmental Policy, 2006

Objectives	*Quality of Current Reporting and Assessment*
Conservation of Critical Environmental Resources	B
Intra-generational Equity: Livelihood Security for the Poor	B
Inter-generational Equity	C
Integration of Environmental Concerns in Economic and Social Development	C
Efficiency in Environmental Resource Use	C
Application of Principles of Good Governance to Environmental Management	B
Enhancement of Resources for Environmental Conservation	C

Source: Column 1 as stated in Ministry of Environment and Forests, Government of India National Environmental Policy, 2006 and column 2 author's qualitative assessment based on Parris T. W, and Kates R.W., 2003.

Action Initiatives Envisaged in NEP

- Institutionalize a holistic and integrated approach to the management of environmental and natural resources, explicitly identifying and integrating environmental concerns in relevant sectoral and cross-sectoral policies, through review and consultation, in line with the National Environment Policy.
- Take steps to adopt and institutionalize techniques for environmental assessment of sector policies and programmes to address any potential adverse impacts, and enhance potential favourable impacts.
- Review the body of existing legislation in order to develop synergies among relevant statutes and regulations, eliminate

obsolescence, and amalgamate provisions with similar objectives, in line with the National Environment Policy. Further, encourage and facilitate review of legislation at the level of state and local governments with a view to ensuring their consistency with this policy.

- Ensure accountability of the concerned levels of government (centre, state, local) in undertaking the necessary legislative changes in a defined time frame, with due regard to the objectives and principles of National Environment Policy, in particular, ensuring the livelihoods and well-being of the poor by ensuring improved access to the necessary environmental resources.

Unless the objective is translated into targets and efforts are made to develop indicators for these targets there would no means to assess and evaluate the outcome of implementation of National Environmental Policy across regions and sectors in India. Given the current level of understanding on the reporting in terms of state of environment at national and state levels, an attempt is being made in Table 1 to grade the quality of reporting and assessment for the stated objective of the National Environmental Policy, 2006. If there are definable targets to broadly indicate the progress on the select objective that has been measured, reported, and assessed routinely on a national or state level that is sufficient to establish a long-term trend receive a letter grade of 'A'. 'B' indicates that the there are no definable targets or indicator exists currently but only estimated through extrapolation, and objectives receive a 'C' when there are no means for assessing the achievement of a stated objective even by using proxies.

Road Mapping the Way Forward

Increasing the Knowledge Base: The current state of knowledge on the influences and impacts of policies and legal framework at international, national and state level on economic operations and environmental and social profile is limited. Similarly, there is a need to enhance understanding of international and national trade along with economic activities on multiple dimensions of sustainable development. While most of these aspects can be analyzed and evaluated with tangible indicators provided efforts are made towards building the knowledge base. There are other intangibles such as culture, values and beliefs etc., which influence sustainability of initiatives. Hence, there is need to develop methods and techniques for diagnosing these dimensions so as to prescribe appropriate solutions. Figure 2 depicts the multidimensional impacts and influences on sustainable development.

Figure 2

Multi-Dimensional Impacts and Influences on Sustainable Development

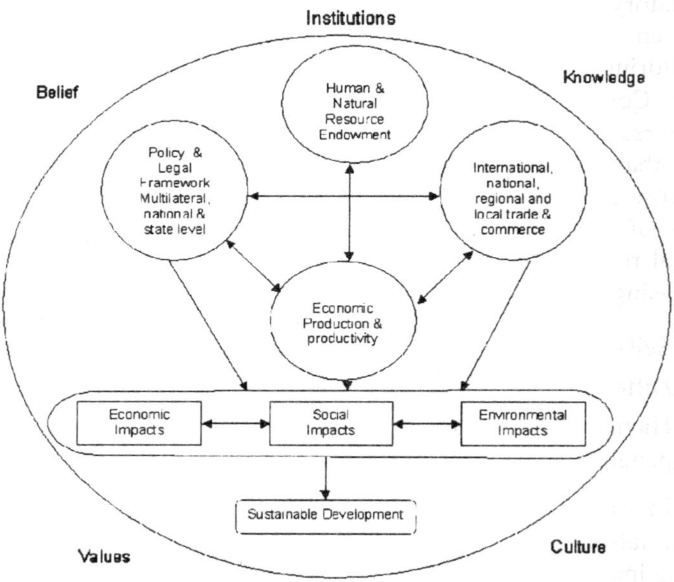

Source: Author's construction

As discussed earlier, there is a large scope of improving environmental management practices across the country. Hence, efforts needs to focused towards increasing institutional and environmental effectiveness in India along with mainstreaming of environment in development sectors at national and state level. This would ensure appropriate top down approach for achieving sustainable development.

Improving Institutional and Environmental Effectiveness

From environmental monitoring and enforcement point of view, if deterrence is the goal to be achieved by environmental enforcement then there should be a clear and firm message of effective enforcement. Delivering such a message is not possible as long as the regulatory agencies dissipate their limited human and financial resources by monitoring and inspecting all regulated units irrespective of their level of compliance. Hence, there is a need for optimizing the available resources by the regulatory agency through an exercise of regulatory prioritization for imposing concentrated regulatory burden. One way of prioritization is to differentiate between compliant firms and non-compliant firms and focus monitoring and enforcement efforts more on the non-compliant firms. Complaint-driven inspections or those targeting suspected violators, for example, are likely to detect higher non-compliance levels than routinely scheduled inspections. Another way is to focus on those facilities that have the highest environmental payoffs per rupee of enforcement effort. Some of the options that environmental regulators can use for reducing monitoring expenses and increasing deterrence include:

- Self-reporting induced by the government/regulator
- Differential monitoring schedule
- Having a penalty policy in place that enables differential penalties based on prior compliance history.

In order to increase their effectiveness and infuse greater accountability, there is a need for developing and using performance indicators for monitoring and enforcement so as to enable evaluation of SPCBs periodically. The rationale for development and usage of environmental compliance and enforcement indicators are:

- Facilitates better monitoring of functioning of SPBs and their functional units
- Enhances greater accountability
- Assists in assessing.

Non-regulatory enforcement tools, such as the impact of information disclosure on firm's behaviour is an important emerging tool of enforcement. The information regarding the monitory sanction imposed on the firm may be of interest to the shareholders or lenders of that firm because it reduces the expected value of the firm and it will affect the share price and bond rating of the firm. There is a need for factoring a positive role of community pressure and other forms of informal sanctions in environmental enforcement programmes of SPCBs.

Decentralized Approach to Environmental Monitoring and Enforcement

There are no instances of decentralization of environmental enforcement in its true spirit but within organizations there are instances of SPCBs decentralizing decision-making to lower levels. Experience from elsewhere shows that decentralization of enforcement to local authorities has enhanced compliance levels but here again the extent is limited as enforcement responsibility is shared between state level agency and local authorities (Cohen, 1998). As the environmental regulations are increasing in their number, the demands of resources for meeting the requirements of law on part of SPCBs have grown substantially in the recent past. Cohen suggests two kinds of innovations for reducing the resource demands on SPCBs and enhancing deterrence among regulators. These innovations include: (1) self-reporting induced by the government, and (2) differential penalties based on prior compliance history. There have been suggestions to the effect that the SPCBs should have access to the EMS self-audits and which can be used in enforcement procedures so as to enhance levels of compliance. But others are of the opinion that giving access to self-audits for regulators might be become counterproductive if made mandatory. Firms in reality would do less audit than they otherwise would conduct. Studies have shown that self-reporting would reduce the costs to regulators on three counts that is when (1) the cost of monitoring/auditing is high, (2) the maximum feasible fine is low, or (3) the desired effort level is high (Malik,

1993). All the above three conditions are applicable to Indian environmental enforcement scenario hence there is a scope of enhancing voluntary self-reporting. To begin with it needs to be extended to those firms, which have fairly robust environmental performance system as observed through its compliance history.

Mainstreaming Environment in Development Sectors

In the last decade, countries across the world started developing national, regional and local strategies for sustainable development and in order to operationalize these strategies they started evaluating and deploying a tool called Strategic Environmental Assessment (SEA). SEA has emerged as a tool for not only integrating social equity and environmental consideration with the developmental processes but also to monitor and evaluate performance of various entities in a transparent and publicly accountable manner. SEA as a tool has been used to a large extent for integrating environmental considerations into the developmental policymaking, planning and programme framing and implementation as it has evolved primarily from widely used EIA tool that attempts to integrate environment in project planning and implementation. But increasingly it is also being used or proposed for usage to integrate social and equity considerations as well so as to align them appropriately with goals of economic growth.

As per the requirements of SEA before focusing on the environment dimension one needs to understand the sectoral baseline and also understand the current policies, programmes and plans in the selected sectors. Activities to be performed in understanding SEA for any given sector includes:

- predicting the significant environmental effects of the plans/programmes;
- identifying mitigation;
- identifying alternatives and their effects;
- consulting the public and authorities with environmental responsibilities;

- reporting how the results of the SEA and consultation responses have been taken into account; and
- monitoring mechanism for environmental effects of the plan and programmes during its implementation.

Strategic Environmental Assessment is considered as a promising avenue for incorporating environmental considerations into the highest levels of development decision-making. At an operational level, SEA will vary with several factors including:

- The level and generality of decision-making (e.g., broad policies versus specific plans);
- The policy sector covered; and
- The type of environmental consequences that can be anticipated, notably whether like effects are direct or indirect, discrete or with spatial linkages.

Timing of the SEA can be broadly categorized into:

- Pre-decision stage; and
- Post-decision stage

While the former is an ideal avenue for integrating environmental and social considerations into policy, plan or programme design as a decision-aiding tool. But the latter is usually used in guiding the implementation of policy. While Figure 3 outlines the stages involved in undertaking SEA for a sector or region, the explanation for each stage and its purpose is outline in Table 2.

Initiatives at the National Level

At the national level, Planning Commission under the chairmanship of Prime Minister is an ideal institutional set up for developing NSDS wherein all the major developmental sectors would not only contribute to its evolution but also participate in development of sector specific targets for achieving them through policy, plan and programme initiatives in a time bound manner so as to deliver its commitments. Ministry of Environment and Forests can be a nodal agency for monitoring and evaluation implementation of NSDS and reporting the same to Planning Commission so that sectoral

Table 2
SEA Stages and its Importance

	SEA Stage	*Purpose of this Stage*
A.	Setting the context, identifying objectives and problems and establishing the baseline:	Document how the plan is affected by outside factors. Suggest ideas for how any inappropriate constraints can be addressed.
	Analysis of the environment protection objectives, established at international, community or national level, which are relevant to the plan.	Streamline the subsequent baseline description, prediction and monitoring stages.
	Establish SEA objectives, indicators and targets.	Provide a base for effects prediction and monitoring.
	Collect relevant information on the environment context as relevant to the plan/programme, and its evolution without the plan/programme.	Focus on key environmental issues and opportunities; help to identify environmental problems, objectives and alternatives.
	Outline the environment characteristics of areas likely to be significantly affected.	
	Outline any existing environment problems which are relevant to the plan including those relating to any areas of a particular environmental importance.	
	Outline the relationship with other relevant plans and programmes.	
B.	Deciding the scope of SEA and developing alternatives:	Help ensure that: The SEA covers key issues.
	Identify relevant alternatives at the strategic level.	The plan better meets the government's aims for more sustainable development.
	Highlight the likely significant effects of the plan and alternatives.	The best plan alternatives(s) is/are considered.
	Consult with environmental authorities when deciding on the scope and level of detail of the information which must be included in the environmental reports.	

Cont'd...

Cont'd...

C.	Assessing the effects of the plan: Forecast the significant effects on the environment of the chosen strategy taking into account the objectives and geographical scope of the plan. Outline the reasons for selecting the alternatives dealt with. Propose measures to prevent, reduce and as fully possible offset any significant adverse effects on the environment of implementing the plan or programme, such measures should be costed and deliverable.	Defensible consideration of all likely significant environment effects. Propose mitigation measures where appropriate. Propose a monitoring programme.
D.	Consultation on the draft plan and the environmental report: Prepare an environmental report in which the likely significant effects on the environment of implementing the plan, and reasonable alternatives taking into account the objectives and geographical scope of the plan. Give environmental authorities and the public an early and effective opportunity within appropriate time-frames to express their opinion on the draft plan and accompanying environmental report before the adoption of the plan. Take consultation results into account. Make available the plan as adopted. Statement summarizing how environmental considerations have been integrated into the plan and how the environmental report, the opinions expressed and the results of consultations entered into pursuant have been taken into light of the other reasonable alternatives dealt with. Proposals for monitoring.	Identify the opinions and concerns of the public and environmental authorities on environmental issues. Show how information and opinions on environmental issues have been considered.

Cont'd...

Cont'd...

E. Monitor the significant effects of implementing the plan on the environment. Decide what needs to be monitored. Identify the information required, including existing sources and gaps. Confirm when the remedial action would be required and identify what remedial actions might be needed. Consider who is responsible for the monitoring activities, when it should be carried out and propose what is the appropriate format for presenting the monitoring results.	Achieve implementation of the plan in accordance with the outcomes of the SEA. Ensure the adverse effects of implementing the plan can be identified and corrective action be taken. Provide information for future SEAs.

Figure 3

Stages for Undertaking SEA in Developmental Sector/Region

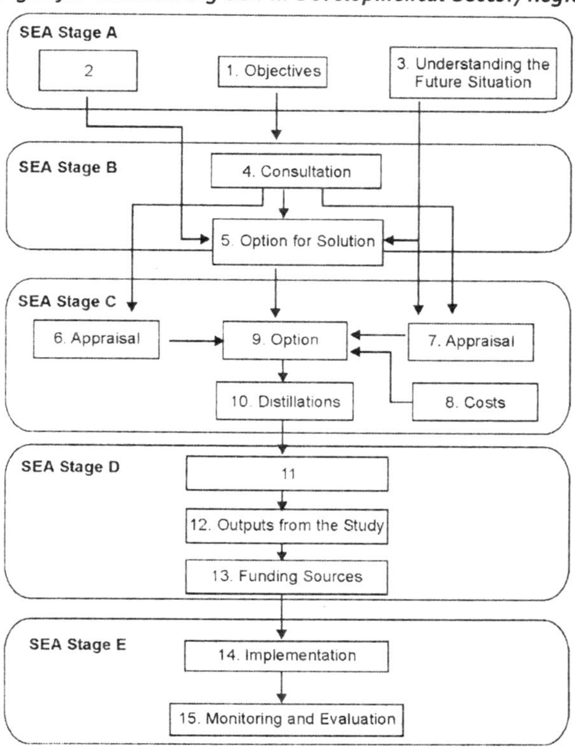

achievements can be reviewed periodically so as to reset the targets and enable continual improvements across the sectors. The State of Environment Reporting initiative can provide the information requirements for developing NSDS at the national level. The information and knowledge gaps in understanding the interface between sectoral developmental activities and environment can be bridged through joint research initiatives of specific ministry and MoEF in consultations with the Planning Commission. The ongoing research on environmental accounting and environmental valuation of the National Statistics Organizations can further the understanding of the extent of resource depletion and degradation due to various sectoral activities and programmes. Sustainable developmental concerns need to be integrated both horizontally and vertically so as to become institutionally effective. Thus, integration of environmental concerns should happen at national, state and local level in different sectors.

Strategic Initiatives at State Level

This broad outline of environmental strategy at the state levels has to be understood in the context of the national environmental framework and sustainable development strategy in India. Any environmental strategy at state level should be derived from the State of Environment (SoE) Report (as shown in Figure 4). While the environmental strategy outlines few specific action initiatives in selected sectors that can be taken up for improving environmental effectiveness of plans and programmes. Action plans provide a key mechanism for securing agreement to the main actions and initiatives, which need to be progressed. A detailed action plan for the regional environment should be attempted wherein an exhaustive list of all possible environmental actions can be prepared departmentwise which require in-depth consultations with the stakeholder departments.

To institutionalize environmental management at state level state government should:

Figure 4
Interfacing SoE Reporting and Strategic Environmental Assessment

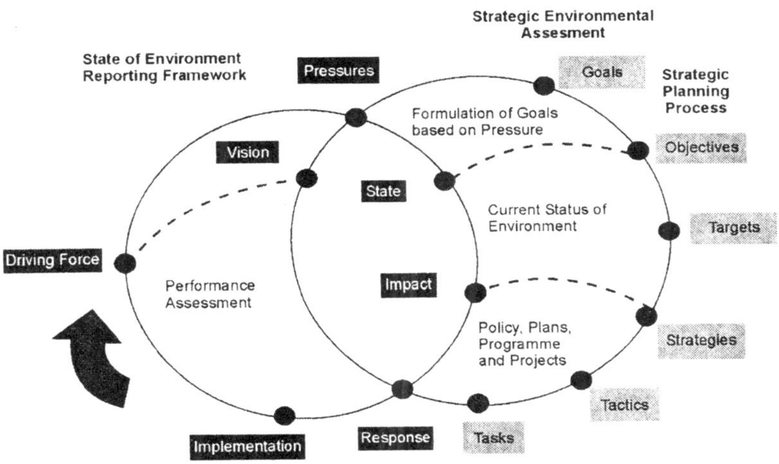

(a) focus on departmentwise environmental coordinators in critical sectors and build their capacities;

(b) attempt to set modest environmental targets (output-based or outcome-based) for select departments;

(c) ensure that a part of the funds allocated to each department on percentage basis is earmarked for environmental activities to be carried out by the respective department;

(d) evolve a mechanism using planning department in coordination with environment department for monitoring and evaluating the achievement of the targets set in an objective and independent manner; and

(e) either Chief Secretary or Chief Minister's office depending on feasibility should periodically review the progress achieved so as to ensure that strategic attention is given to the environmental dimension in the state planning and programme implementing system.

Apart from this, interest needs to be generated in officials of various departments/agencies by conducting annual departmentwise or cross-departmental thematic environmental workshops especially in departments like energy, irrigation, urban transport, tourism, forestry, agriculture etc. While it is recognized that environmental education plays a vital role in moulding the culture and value system of society towards environment but given its long-term gains limited focus is given to this dimension in the planning process. It needs to be recognized that environmental education is an essential part of the process of developing a more sustainable society. It provides an avenue to generate an understanding and an appreciation of the value of both the intrinsic nature of the environment—its ecological mechanisms and balances its effects on human development. Hence, strategic attention to this dimension is critical from sustainable development perspective.

Conclusions

Indian development strategy needs to be aligned with its resource endowment and using appropriate prices for renewable and non-renewable resources as a prerequisite for improving the sustainability of its development. Experience from developed world suggests that unless it is mandated through tools like SEA, it is difficult to integrate environment in the developmental sectors processes. Evidences from energy, transport and urban sectors demonstrates that neither regulations nor prices alone are sufficient conditions for bringing out required changes in the process and systems. Changing the policies, plans and programmes along with financial and institutional changes can contribute towards integrating environment and social aspects into developmental process. But prevailing well-entrenched interests, institutional culture, belief and values people manning the institutions determine effectiveness of the progress towards sustainable development. Hence, initiatives at national and state levels that are evolved through high levels of public participation can give strategic attention to sustainable developmental concerns which can serve as immediate steps.

References

Auty, R.M., "Natural Resources, Developmental Models and Sustainable Development", International Institute for Economic and Development, Discussion Paper No. 1–3, June, 2003.

Brandon, C. and Hommann, K. (1995), "The Cost of Inaction: Valuing the Economy-wide Cost of Environmental Degradation in India", Asia Environment Division, World Bank, 17 October, 1995.

Brown, R. Lester, *Plan B 2.0 Rescuing a Planet under Stress and a Civilization in Trouble,* W.W. Norton and Co., New York, 2006.

Cohen, M.A. (1998), "Monitoring and Enforcement of Environmental Policy", downloaded from http://www.worldbank.org/nipr/work_paper/cohen/cohen.pdf on June 28, 2004.

Esty, Daniel C., Levy, Marc A., Tanja, Srebotnjak and Alexander, de Sherbinin (2005), *2005 Environmental Sustainability Index: Benchmarking National Environmental Stewardship,* New Haven, Conn.: Yale Center for Environmental Law and Policy.

Jha, Raghbendra and Whalley, John, "The Environmental Regime in Developing Countries", NBER Working Paper 7305, August, 1999. sourced from http://www.nber.org/papers/w7305.

Kolanu, T.R. and Jhamthani, R.C., "Alternatives Economic Instruments for Industrial Pollution Prevention in India", International Workshop on Economic Instruments for Industrial Pollution Control in India, New Delhi, June 13–15, 2001.

Kolanu, T.R., "National Guidelines for State of Environment Reporting in India", Administrative Staff College of India, Unpublished report submitted to Ministry of Environment and Forests, Government of India, September, 2004.

McKean, R.N. (1980), "Enforcement Costs in Environmental and Safety Regulation", Policy-Analysis, 6(3), 269–89.

Ministry of Environment and Forests, *National Environmental Policy, 2006*, MoEF, Government of India, June, 2006.

Ministry of Environment and Forests, *Prior Environmental Clearance Notification*, MoEF, Government of India, September, 2006.

OECD (2001), *The DAC Strategies for Sustainable Development-International Development*, OECD, Paris, France.

OECD (2002), *Governance for Sustainable Development: Five OECD Case Studies*, OECD, Paris, France.

Pargal, S., Mani, M. and Haq, M., *Inspections and Emissions in India: Puzzling Survey Evidence of Industrial Water Pollution*, The World Bank, August 1997.

Parris, T.M. and Kates, R.W. (2003), *Characterizing a Sustainability Transition: Goals, Targets, Trends, and Driving Forces*, PNAS, Vol. 100, No. 14, July 8, 2003, sourced from www.pnas.org_cgi_doi_10.1073_pnas. 1231336100.

Pearce, David, "Conceptual Framework for Analysing Distributive Impacts of Environmental Policies", Prepared for the OECD Environment Directorate Workshop on the Distribution of Benefits and Costs of Environmental Policies, Paris, March, 2003.

Shamsul, Haque M., "Recent Transition in Governance in South Asia: Contexts, Dimensions, and Implications", *International Journal of Public Administration*, Vol. 24, Issue: 12, 2001.

UNDP 2004, *Framework and Strategies for Sustainable Development: Practical Note*, UNDP, 20 April, 2004.

4 Privatization of Water

Impact on Development

Vinita Pandey

Water undeniably is one of the most vital sources for survival of mankind. The United Nations maintains that water is a social and cultural good and not merely economic commodity. Today, one of the largest concerns around the world is the lack of freshwater for drinking and cooking. It is estimated that over one billion people, or about one-sixth of the world's population, do not have access to fresh water; of these one billion, the vast majority are living in developing nations. Although water is one of the most common resources on the planet, only 2.5 per cent of it can actually be consumed, and the rest is salt water. Of that 2.5 per cent, two-thirds is confined to glaciers and permanent snow cover. Only a fraction of the world's water is liquid freshwater, and it is increasingly the subject of conflict and strife as it is scarce. Global consumption of water is doubling every 20 years, more than twice the rate of human population growth. At present more than one billion people on earth lack access to fresh drinking water. By the year 2025, the demand for freshwater is expected to rise to 56 per cent above what currently available water can deliver, if current trends persist.

The United Nations Department of Economic and Social Affairs (DESA), Division for Sustainable Development Agenda 21 Chapter 18, uphold "Water is needed in all aspects of life. The general objective is to make certain that adequate supplies of water of good quality are maintained for the entire population of this planet, while preserving the hydrological, biological and chemical functions of ecosystems, adapting human activities within the capacity limits of nature and combating vectors of water-related diseases. Innovative technologies, including the improvement of indigenous technologies, are needed to fully utilize limited water resources and to safeguard those resources against pollution" (Clause 18.2).

Water Stress

By the year 2025, the demand for freshwater is expected to rise to 56 per cent. With this constant change mankind is facing water stress and water scarcity. A country is said to experience 'water stress' when annual water supplies drop below 1,700 cubic metres per person. At levels between 1,700 and 1,000 cubic metres per person, periodic or limited water shortages can be expected. When annual water supplies drop below 1,000 cubic metres per person, the country faces water scarcity. India is under the category of water stress countries.

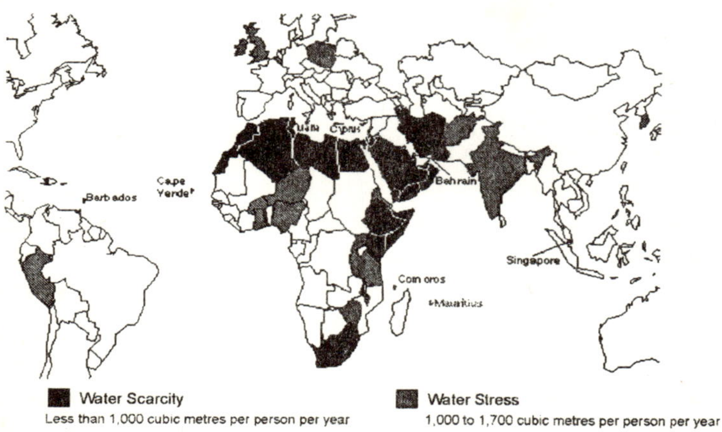

The widespread scarcity, gradual destruction and aggravated pollution of freshwater resources in many world regions, along with the progressive encroachment of incompatible activities, demand integrated water resources planning and management. Such integration must cover all types of interrelated freshwater bodies, including both surface water and groundwater, and duly consider water quantity and quality aspects.

The extent to which water resources development contributes to economic productivity and social well-being is not usually appreciated, although all social and economic activities rely heavily on the supply and quality of freshwater. As populations and economic activities grow, many countries are rapidly reaching conditions of water scarcity or facing limits to economic development. Water demands are increasing rapidly, with 70–80 per cent required for irrigation, less than 20 per cent for industry and a mere 6 per cent for domestic consumption. The holistic management of freshwater as a finite and vulnerable resource, and the integration of sectoral water plans and programmes within the framework of national economic and social policy, are of paramount importance for action in the 1990s and beyond.

The increasing pressure on the infrastructure due to population explosion, growing consumption of water (for various purposes including drinking, irrigation and agriculture, construction, industrial and other purposes) and scarcity of water has made water a highly significant factor for development. Though India as a nation has made major leaps and progress in various sectors, lakhs of people remain thirsty or are forced to consume polluted water. Water, which is one of the basic rights of human beings, is increasingly becoming an issue of conflict not only between the nations but also between the states of a nation. A very important perspective related to the water conflict has been added by the argument of privatizing it like many other sectors.

The Present Water Management System

The ecological variation of India can be understood by the simple fact that it is divided in to 15 ecological regions and the similar diversity is reflected in its various sources of water (rainfall, groundwater and surface water). The average rainfall in India is 1,170 mm, however intense geographical diversities lead to varied rainfall levels with extreme variation in Cherrapunji in North Eastern India and parts of Rajasthan and Gujarat. The unplanned exploitation of groundwater is leading to falling water table between 1 and 3 metre every year.

Lacuna in Present System

The contemporary water system is purely driven by the supply objective and not by offering appropriate services to the existing connections. The operations and maintenance is not upto the standards leading to poor quality of service. Further, the public expenditure is not made accountable, political intervention, lack of transparency and accountability make things difficult. The mismanagement of water resources, inappropriate policies on water management and faulty implementation of the same has brought about tough challenges not only for the governments to manage but also for the common man. The increasing population, mounting pressure on the infrastructure and unplanned constructions on the various water resource beds have made the situation grave. The geographical diversity has been instrumental in inappropriate distribution of water resources, which has been pointed out earlier.

The water management service includes collection, purification, distribution of water, and waste water treatment in a community. Traditionally, this service has been provided by the local governmental infrastructure such as the municipality or local city council.

Introducing Privatization of Water

The solution to water crisis suggested by World Bank, IMF is 'Privatization of Water'. Water privatization involves transferring of water control and/or water management services to private companies. Water Privatization Policy was articulated by World Bank in a 1992 paper entitled "Improving Water Resources

Management". The Bank believes that water availability at low or no cost is uneconomic and inefficient. Even the poor should pay. As the World Bank states, "When water services are reliable, the poor are willing to pay for them, and when service is not reliable, the poor pay more for less, typically from street vendors. As pointed out in the 'World Development Report 1992', the poor need to be provided with a wider range of options so they can choose the level of water services for which they are willing to pay, thereby giving suppliers a financial stake in meeting the needs of the poor. Fee schedules can be structured so that consumers receive a limited amount of water at a low cost and pay a higher fee for additional water."

In her book *Water Wars,* Vandana Shiva states, "Water must be free for sustenance needs. Since nature gives water to us free of cost, buying and selling it for profit violates our inherent right to nature's gift and denies the poor of their human rights. Water is a common … . It cannot be owned as private property and sold as a commodity". How can one justify claiming water as their own through contractual agreement while letting another human beings go thirsty? Water is a common because it is the basis of all life. Water rights are natural rights and thus are usufructuary rights, meaning that water can be used, but not owned. As far-fetched as water ownership may seem, it is happening at an increasing rate around the globe.

As Lalita Sridhar and Shripad Dharmadhikary, earlier associated with the Narmada Bachao Andolan and presently the Founder-Director of the Manthan Adhyayan Kendra, Badwani, Madhya Pradesh argue that water as a private commodity has been in existence in India since a long time. Groundwater is practically private property. This unlimited access has also given rise to well-developed water markets, e.g., in North Gujarat, many industries, even large residential colonies pump out their own groundwater. Similarly, water supply through private tankers too has been a part and parcel of Indian life since long. Whether it is handcart or bullock cart mounted drums, or truck/tractor tankers, private supply of water is common. These tankers supply water to individuals, big colonies, and hotels and to many others, especially under water 'scarcity' conditions.

There have been in past one decade certain new developments, which characterize a deep shift in the nature of the water privatization. The change is from the individual private operators who were somewhere related to public sector to multinational corporations and water giants like Vivendi Environment and Suez-Lyonnaise des Eaux. Both are based in Paris but are spreading their empires worldwide. The French water giants have water interests in 120 countries.

It is vital to note here that privatization of water has been in vogue and practise in different forms and three well-known models of privatization are as follows:

- *Service Contracts:* In this model, public authority retains overall responsibility for the operation and maintenance of the system, and contracts out specific components. Service contracts last 1–3 years and include services such as meter reading, billing and maintenance. While public ownership is maintained and community accountability structures remain in place, the transparency of operation can be limited. Contracts are often not openly negotiated and regulation and oversight is usually lacking.
- *(Design), Build, Operate, Own and Transfer or (D) BOOT:* This model of privatization is usually used for system infrastructure development such as water treatment plants that require significant finance. The private operator is required to finance, construct, operate and maintain the facility for a specific period of time (usually more than 20 years). At the end of the term, the infrastructure may be turned over to the municipality or the contract is renewed. This model is more prevalent in developing countries. Examples of (D) BOOT include Tiruppur Project in Tamil Nadu, India and Cochabamba experience in Bolivia.
- *Divestiture:* In this model, the government or public authority awards full ownership and responsibility of the water system including the water source to a private operator under a

regulatory regime. This is also done in the form of 10–20 year renewable contracts on the entire system. The government moves operation to private hands thus improving efficiency. Competition is limited through the process of bids on the divestiture. The private sector firm is then expected to take the risks and recoup investment/profits. This model cedes tremendous power over an essential resource to corporations. Examples of divestiture include the Rasmada scheme, under which a 22-year lease over a stretch of the Shiv Nath River in Chattisgarh was accorded to Radius water Inc.

Most of the privatization that has been done in India follows the (D) BOOT model. The Government of India policy on water maintains the following:

"Private sector participation may help in introducing innovative ideas, generating financial resources and introducing corporate management and improving service efficiency and accountability to users." *Water Policy of Government of India*, April 1, 2002.

Why Privatization?

The various policies and framework of government has undergone significant changes in the post 1991 India. In fact liberalization, privatization and globalization are being viewed as panacea for any problem area and so it equally applies to water.

The rationale for privatization of the water sector is much the same as for the rest of LPG. The logic goes like this—governments no longer have the funds required for the huge investments necessary in sectors like power, water, roads etc. There is little internal generation of resources due to below cost supply of water. It is only the private sector that can bring in the finances required. The following aspects have been considered to justify privatization of water:

- No funds for huge investment and public sector: Experiences give a very general impression to be inefficient, corrupt and lack of transparency.

- Private sector, especially the global players will bring in superior technology, huge capital, better management and accountancy practices.
- The political interference, the negligence, diversion of resources, favouritism and nepotism—all at the cost of the performance and poor gets affected.
- Commodification of water shall bring in market forces (supply and demand) to set the water tariff, which shall lead to reduced water consumption and promote water conservation.

Thus, to be precise, supporters of privatization deem that privatization shall help in wiping the evils of inefficiency, corruption, red tapism, nepotism and bring in more accountability and transparency. But what is the assurance that it shall actually help the alleviate the problem. Moreover, the profit motive shall be guiding the most important natural right to water. How far that would be right?

Threats from Privatization and Impact on Development

The World Bank has recently initiated water sector reforms, aimed primarily at privatization of water resources and commercialization of water management. The privatization policy recommends commercializing operations at all levels, private investment, substantial increase in water prices, increase in agricultural power tariffs, and creation of water markets. The lack of welfare motive, predominance of profit making approach and increase in power tariffs shall very negatively affect the farming sector and medium and low-class farmers who are committing suicides. The Indian economy is highly dependent on agriculture which depends on water. Apart from rainfall if other sources of water are privatized the situation of Indian farming sector would be grimmer.

There are many potential risks and threats, which are emerging and shall consolidate over a period of time due to privatization of water. Some of them are discussed below. The following have been liberally drawn from Public Citizen Website "Top 10 Reasons to Oppose Water Privatization".

Commodification of Water and Impact on Ecology

The World Bank estimates the potential water market at $800 billion and $2 billion in India. Thus, basic human right becomes a commodity driven by market forces inevitably hiking of water tariffs—making the water service unaffordable for the poor. The policies of privatization imposed through the World Bank and rules of trade liberalization being negotiated in the World Trade Organization (WTO) under the General Agreement on Trade in Services (GATS) are rules and conditionality that create corporate states—states that usurp resources from people for meeting vital needs and put them in the hands of private corporations for making profits through the privatization of essential services. The business logic of sustainable development is that population growth and economic development will apply increasing pressure on natural resource markets. Monsanto plans to earn revenues of $420 million and net income of $63 million by 2008 from its water business in India and Mexico. By the year 2010, it is projected that about 2.5 billion people in the world will lack access to safe drinking water. At least 30 per cent of the population in China, India, Mexico, and the US is expected to face severe water stress. By the year 2025, the supply of water in India will be 700 cubic km per year, while the demand is expected to rise to 1,050 units. Control over this scarce resource will of course be a source of guaranteed profits.

The crisis of pollution and depletion of water resources is viewed by Monsanto as a business opportunity. For Monsanto, 'sustainable development' means the conversion of an ecological crisis into a market of scarce resources. The World Bank emphasizes on shift from a 'supply-oriented' to a 'demand-oriented' approach. Thus, the demands of the economically powerful will override the needs of the poor.

Price Hikes are Unaffordable for the Poor

Water privatization has perpetually led to price hikes in almost all the areas in the world where water has been privatized. Since substantial costs are involved in water harnessing, purification and distribution systems. For such expensive projects, water companies borrow private money, which is subject to high interest rates from financiers and state taxation. The companies recover their costs and expenses by charging the consumer. Not only is the capital cost divided among all the consumers but also the interest, taxes and overheads on the capital. Thus, the consumer is forced to bear the burden of higher payments on company loans. In contrast, tax-free public financing results in low costs for such projects in community owned or state controlled water systems. Increased consumer fees for water can make safe water unaffordable for the impoverished and vulnerable populations.

As Vandana Shiva points out that "... These are recipes for conversion of water into a tradeable commodity rather than a life support base. Privatization will aggravate the water crisis, because given the inequalities between rich and poor, industry and agriculture, urban and rural, water markets will take the water from the poor to the rich, from impoverished rural areas to affluent urban enclaves. It will also lead to overexploitation of water, because when access to water is determined by the market and not by limits of renewability, the water cycle will be systematically violated and the water crisis will deepen. Local community management is a precondition for both consumption and equitable use". Ignoring limits of water availability and the conservation imperative, the Bank recommends a shift from a 'supply-oriented' to a 'demand-oriented' approach. Demands of the economically powerful will therefore override the needs of the poor and the limits of nature. Partial application of this logic through World Bank lending is not the root of the present crisis. Full implementation of the logic of privatization will not reverse the crisis; it will aggravate it.

The first consequence of privatization is almost inevitably the hiking of water tariffs—making the water service unaffordable for the poor. This is the experience from all parts of the world. In Ho Chi Minh City, the rates went up by seven times. In Cochabamba, rates shot up so that the average worker was required to shell out 25 per cent of his/her salary in water charges. In Metro Manila, where the company Mynilad was given the concession under the condition of supply at Peso 4.96 per cubic metre, the company hiked the prices to 15.46 pesos and then was asking for 30. When this was not granted, it walked out of the concessions, leaving the city high and dry. Moreover, the private company is in the business for its own profits—and is not going to be considerate to those who cannot afford the high rates. They will simply be disconnected. For example, in Guinea, where prices rose by 650 per cent, taking them even higher than rates in London and Paris, non-payment resulted in disconnection of about 10,000 connections, roughly one-third of the total clientele. In South Africa, millions of people are reported to be affected by disconnections due to non-payment.

In France, customer fees increased by 150 per cent as a result of privatization, but water quality deteriorated. A French government report revealed that more than 5.2 million citizens received 'bacterially unacceptable' water. In England, water rates increased by 450 per cent, profits of water companies increased by 692 per cent, and salaries of CEOs increased 708 per cent. Meanwhile, the number of customers who have been disconnected from water services as a result of the price hikes has increased by 50 per cent. Dysentery increased sixfold, and the British Medical Association had to condemn water privatization because of its health impacts. In Argentina, the state-run water company, Obras Samitarias de la Naceon, was sold to Aguas Argentinas, a subsidiary of Suez-Lyonnaise des Eaux. The IFC, an arm of the World Bank, provided a $172.5 million loan to Aguas Argentinas in 1994. A subsidiary of the French company got a 30-year rural water contract. It doubled the rates, but failed to provide clean water. The company was forced to pull out because people refused to pay their bills (Source: http:// www.thirdworldtraveler.com).

Serious Implications on Rural Development

Around 72 per cent of Indian population lives in rural areas. Private companies have little incentive to service the dispersed, low-density populations in the rural areas. Vast majority of the Indian poor live in rural areas dependent on agriculture which in turn depends on water resources. *What Happens to Rural Development?* Private sector does not entertain direct or indirect subsidies, which are vital for water supply to the poor. According to one of the estimates, private services to provide water can reach only to 17 per cent of the poor in the country. *What about the rest?*

Unsustainable Water Mining

After water becomes a saleable commodity and a corporation is given sole rights to a body of water, then it is within the corporation's rights to mine as much water as it deems fit. Furthermore, in an effort to maximize profits, if the corporation mines an environmentally unsustainable amount of water and depletes the water body at a rate faster than it is replenished, then the government officials and the affected population can do very little to legally prevent the corporation from doing so. The haphazard mining of groundwater by Coca Cola in the Khammam district of Andhra Pradesh, Athur village near Chennai and Plachimada in Kerala. Residents from villages in the Palghat district in Kerala surrounding Coke's Greenfield soft-drink bottling factory in Plachimada say that Coke's indiscriminate water mining has dried up many wells and contaminated the rest.

Coca Cola's bottling plant was set up in 1999 in the middle of fertile agricultural land, with proximity to a number of reservoirs and irrigation canals. Coke's mining of more than 1 million litres of groundwater per day has parched the lands of some 2000 people within 1.2 miles of the factory. Due to the indiscriminate mining, the groundwater has become contaminated with excessive calcium and magnesium from the dissolution of limestone that is associated with the groundwater deposit. Nearly 100 people have reported recurring stomach aches, which they relate to the brackish and milky white water that they are being forced to drink. This is a very serious health hazard and in the long run can prove to be much more hazardous.

Creation of Water Monopolies

Fortune magazine has labelled water as the 'oil of the 21st century'. With such huge profits at stake, corporations around the world strive to ensure that water as a commodity remains in private control. The water corporations are aided and supported in their effort by financial institutions such as the World Bank, WTO and IMF, which enforce many free trade agreements and structural adjustment programmes on developing countries as a prerequisite for a 'developmental' loan. A water corporation can use one of the many free trade treaties to take legal action against the government for withdrawing from an agreement to privatize water systems. Although this has not yet happened in India, there are numerous instances of lawsuits filed by water corporations against local governments that backed out of a contract in countries with a longer history of water privatization. It has been seen that it eventually ends in a water monopoly sanctioned by the government agencies.

Water Quality Compromised

Corporations in search of profits can compromise on water quality in order to reduce costs. This is especially true in a country such as India, where the water quality regulatory boards do not have the teeth to enforce their standards. There have been numerous instances of outbreak of epidemics due to poor quality of water. As discussed earlier, Coca Cola's indiscriminate mining of groundwater has contaminated groundwater deposits with excessive amounts of calcium and magnesium in the Plachimada district in Kerala, which has led to health problems among the villagers in the area. In Walkerton, Canada, seven people died and several became ill as a result of E-coli contamination in the drinking water. The private company, A&L Laboratories, contracted to test the drinking water knew of the contamination but regulations intended to encourage privatization ensured that company was not required to alert the government. In India, the bottled water industries and cola industry have been shown to have high pesticide levels in their products. These are classic examples of how private companies cannot be expected to provide quality without regulation. While privatization of essential services is pushed, regulation of these services is being removed through budget cuts.

In March 1999, the Natural Resource Defence Council studied 103 brands of bottled water to find that bottled water is no safer than tap water. One-third of the brands contained arsenic and E. coli; one-fourth contained merely bottle tap water. In India, a study on bottled water published in the January/February 1998 issue of the Ahmedabad-based Consumer Education and Research Centre magazine *Insight* said that of the 13 known brands, only three conformed to all the specifications. None of the brands were free of bacteria, though some brands claimed to be 'germ free' and 100 per cent bacteria free.

Potential Export of Bulk Water

Privatization opens the door to bulk water exports as control over this scarce resource is transferred from local communities to profit minded global corporations. Bulk water exports will have disastrous ecological and environmental consequences. For instance, the huge market for drinking water in the perpetually water starved city of Chennai has prompted several private companies to mine the surrounding villages for groundwater. The residents of Mathur Village in North Chennai sued several bottled water companies in 1995 for illegally extracting groundwater. By the time the case was taken up in 1999, more than 60 private companies supplying water by tanker trucks had sunk additional illegal wells in Mathur.

Corruption and Lack of Transparency

The lack of accountability and transparency in giving of service contracts to private corporations has been apparent in Indian scenario. The Enron scandal—in which the Maharashtra government awarded Enron a contract for generation and supply of 695 MW of electric power—has epitomized the allegations of bribes and 'kickbacks' that have plagued practically every major service contract awarded by governments in India. In many cases, the government guarantees against any losses incurred by the water corporation by setting up hedge funds for such purposes or assuring regular payments to the corporations for fixed amounts of water regardless of actual usage.

Furthermore, the potential for huge profits and long-term monopoly over supply of an essential resource such as water has doubly increased the incentives for private corporations active in this sector to offer bribes in order to secure contracts. Executives of many water corporations have been convicted for bribing government officials worldwide.

Public Apathy and Lack of Public Debate

Often, there is little or no public debate on the project before the decision to privatize is taken. As a result, infrastructure and capital-intensive project contracts are awarded even where there is no need for such projects. For example, in Delhi, the private company Degremont is planning to build pipelines from Tehri Dam for domestic water supply when rainwater harvesting has been shown to work. Similarly, the water being brought to Gujarat from the Narmada valley has cost the state more than Rs 100 million. The government is planning on higher taxation to recover this cost. Alternate water harvesting schemes have been implemented by NGOs in these areas at a fraction of the cost. Such massive infrastructures where they are not needed are the root cause of the inefficiency and are bound to be a problem with privatization as well.

The arguments given above highlight the dangers and risks involved in water privatization. While government management of water resources is partly responsible for the water crisis we face today, privatization will at best compound the problem. There is a clear need for alternate models which offer equitable, sustainable and efficient management of water resources. Such models exist all over the world and have been quite successful in their implementation and public acceptance. The privatization of water services is the first step in privatization of water. The US water market, estimated at $90 billion, is the largest in the world. Vivendi is investing heavily to control it. In March 1999, it purchased US Filter Corporation for more than $6 billion and formed the largest water corporation in North America, with projected revenues of $12 billion.

Case Studies on Privatization of Water

Shivnath River, Chattisgarh

The Chattisgarh State Industries Development Corporation (CSIDC), which is in charge of industrial development in the state, commissioned the project to meet the demand on water in the Borai Industrial Area situated on the banks of the Shivnath—a non-perennial river. As part of the project, a 23.6 km stretch of the river was ceded to Radius Water through a 22-year renewable contract, under which the company had absolute monopoly over the stretch of river water. In return, Radius Water would provide water to the CSIDC from the Shivnath during the lean 6 months. The company built an integrated water supply system to control the water flow automatically depending on the level of the Shivnath and set the water tariff at substantially lower rates than that charged by the neighbouring states of Madhya Pradesh and Maharashtra. The project was initially hailed as a success by the government. However, the catch was that the agreement assured Radius Water of payment for a minimum of four million litres of water per day by the state government, regardless of the amount of water used and irrespective of whether the CSIDC recovers this amount from the industries. The CSIDC lost Rs 12.9 millions between December 2000 and June 2002. Furthermore, Radius Water's monopolistic deal with CSIDC and the water resources department covered groundwater as well in an 18 km radius covering the Borai Industrial Area. The company promptly prohibited fishing in the stretch of the river and also charged local farmers for access to water from tubewells. Ultimately, bowing to pressure from several NGOs and adverse media reports, the government had to scrap the deal.

Sonia Vihar Issue, New Delhi

Degremont—a subsidiary of the French water giant Suez—has been awarded a Rs 2 billion contract under a 10-year BOT agreement with the Delhi Jal Board (DJB) for a drinking water treatment plant in Sonia Vihar near New Delhi. The water treatment plant is expected to yield 635 million litres of drinking water a day. While Degremont is getting the raw water for free through pipelines from the Upper Ganga canal of the Tehri Dam project (near Muradnagar, Uttar Pradesh) the amount it will get as a fee for treating the water will be much in excess of what the DJB will charge the consumers when selling the water. The DJB is also providing Degremont with land, electricity and treatment cost. At the same time, Degremont has been kept free from transmission losses and revenue collection and has also been assured the purchase of treated water and productivity incentives once the plant begins operations. The Sonia Vihar plant has been plagued by controversies since its inception. The leader of the opposition party and some ruling party members have levelled allegations of corruption and irregularities in the allotment of contract to Degremont. A Delhi-based NGO, Research Foundation for Science and Technology, has accused the Delhi Jal Board of wasteful practises.

The experiences of various developed and developing countries are no different. For instance, while responding to the World Bank structural adjustment policies, Bolivia privatized the water subsystem in its third largest city Cochabamba in 1999 and granted a 40-year concession to run the water system to Italy-based international water company and US-based Bechtel, with an agreement that user fees would remain the same in dollars. So every time the local currency fell, the price would spiral. Soon after bagging the contract, the companies raised the water tariff to $20 per month and imposed permits for collecting rainwater on roofs. For the majority with earnings of less than $65 per month, the increased tariff meant less water access.

Mass local protests organized into a coalition in defence of water and life. After weeks of intense protests, the government cancelled the contract with private companies. Bechtel is now suing the nation of Bolivia for $25 million dollars for cancelling the contract.

In UK, privatization came with huge government subsidies. The government converted the regional water authority bodies into private profit-making entities, wrote off $8 billion in debt of the water companies before privatization and gave a further $2.6 billion to help the newly formed companies meet new EU environmental requirements. To complete the deal, the new companies were guaranteed private monopolies for 25 years and were given a special exemption from paying taxes on their profits. Following privatization, there was an unprecedented water price hike of over 50 per cent in the first 4 years; the corresponding rate of household disconnections due to non-payment also rose threefold (12% of total households). The companies were allowed to increase prices on the basis of their projected capital investment to improve infrastructure. Once the price rises were agreed in 1995, many companies rapidly discovered reasons not to follow the investment forecast, and announced 'capital efficiencies', which enabled them to award the money not spent on investments as increased dividends to shareholders. These were substantial amounts, between £50m and £100m for Thames water, North West water, and Yorkshire water (now Kelda), for example. Furthermore, as per the Environmental Agency's 2000 report, seven of top ten polluters in the country are water companies.

Alternative Solutions

The privatization of water is being sought owing to water crisis and mismanagement in the existing system. Thus, alternative solutions should also concentrate on creating water surplus. Some of them are:

Rainwater Harvesting

The harvesting of rainwater involves the collection of water from surfaces on which rain falls, and subsequently storing this water for later use. Normally, water is collected from the roofs of buildings and stored in rainwater tanks or allowed to recharge groundwater and thus providing a perennial source of water. In India, with its monsoons, rainwater harvesting experience is millennial, born of local wisdom and is widely used today. It is scientific and the focus of innovation in the present, participatory and the basis of people's movements, and the best way to a non-scarce future.

The world's freshwater shortages result more from uneven distribution of water over time and space than from absolute scarcity. Even in some of the world's highest rainfall areas, rain falls in concentrated periods followed by prolonged dry spells, so users must capture rainwater when it is abundant to use later when it is scarce. Similarly, even in some of the driest areas, occasional intense rainfall generates runoff that can be captured and stored for subsequent use. For example, harvesting only 100 mm of rainfall over a one-hectare plot would yield 1 million litres of water. Ancient water harvesting systems throughout the world took advantage of this principle to smooth inter temporal variations in water availability, making human settlement possible in a wide variety of ecosystems.

Local water harvesting declined with the development of large systems in which water is transported hundreds of miles through canals and pipes or pumped from great depths below the ground. However, growing scarcity and intersectoral competition for water, along with groundwater depletion and the problems facing major surface water control systems, have raised interest in revitalizing water harvesting systems that capture rainwater wherever it falls.

Water harvesting refers to the small-scale concentration, collection, storage, and use of rainwater runoff for both domestic and agricultural use. This definition implies that the catchment area from which the water is drawn is larger than the command area, where it is collected and used. The ratio of catchment to command is inversely related to the amount and intensity of rainfall, the impermeability of soil, and the slope of the land on which it falls. Rainfall intensity is particularly important, since intense storms generate the most runoff. A watershed is an area that drains to a common point. It may be managed for various objectives, depending on local needs, including capturing runoff, minimizing erosion, and reducing nonpoint source pollution. In management of small watersheds, capturing runoff for local use is conceptually equivalent to harvesting water. This brief encompasses all small-scale, local systems for capturing runoff from rainfall. Water harvesting systems either concentrate water into a storage reservoir or apply water directly to the soil in the cropped area. Both types of systems can vary in scale from a few square metres benefiting a single household to a few square kilometres serving a larger group of people.

There are success stories of urban rainwater harvesting in Chennai, Delhi and Gujarat. The amendments in municipal laws and strong initiatives by the non-government organizations have created an innovative pathway to fight water crisis.

Watershed Management, Kothapally, Andhra Pradesh

Kothapally village in the Ranga Reddy district of Andhra Pradesh is blessed with rich black soil but little rain. The village's watershed management programme, which is run by a consortium of partners under the leadership of the International Crop Research Institute (ICRISAT), has become a model for community involvement in watershed development. The consortium includes the Government of Andhra Pradesh, the Drought Prone Area Program, the Central Research Institute for Dry Land Agriculture, the National Remote Sensing Agency, and the Farmer's Association. Under this project, several techniques for soil and water conservation and crop improvement were implemented to the benefit of the small farmers. These farmers saw the value of water harvesting and joined the consortium of project partners in constructing 13 check dams and 51 mini percolation tanks, which has increased water levels, expanded green cover and enhanced the productivity of crops.

2. Efficient and professional services through governance and regulation.

3. It is important to find innovative ways to address the physical constraints to infrastructure in low-income areas.
4. Need to understand local characteristics, evolve a suitable policy and incorporate explicit pro-poor provisions and incentives in the contracts and find an 'appropriate tariff and subsidy design'.

Participation of Farmers and Voluntary Agencies

Efforts should be made to involve farmers progressively in various aspects of management of irrigation systems, particularly in water distribution and collection of water rates. Assistance of voluntary agencies should be enlisted in educating the farmers in efficient water use and water management. A classic example of people's participation is Ralegaon Siddhi, Maharashtra. In 1975, when Anna Hazare retired from the army and went back to his village in Ahmednagar district, Maharashtra, he found the village reeling under drought, poverty, debt, and unemployment. He decided to mobilize the people and with the collective support of all the villagers, he began to introduce changes. Today, Ralegaon Siddhi is being taken as a role model for other villages by the Maharashtra government and by other states too. Massive tree plantation has been undertaken, and hills have been terraced to check erosion. Large canals with ridges on either side have been dug to retain rainwater. As a result, the water table in this area is now considerably higher and the wells and tube wells are never dry, making it possible to raise three crops a year where only one was possible before.

Training

A perspective plan for standardized training should be an integral part of water resources development ... it should cover training in information systems, sectoral planning, projects planning and formulation, project management, operation of projects and their physical structures and systems and the management of the water distribution systems. The training should extend to all the categories of personnel involved in these activities as also the farmers.

Conclusion

It is an undisputed fact that 'Water is life'. The gamut of discussion around privatization of water owes its origin to water scarcity and mismanagement by the existing operators. However, it would be highly appropriate to state that privatization of water necessarily need not ensure meeting the requirements of the whole society for varied purposes of drinking, agriculture, industrial etc. On the contrary, the experiences of privatization of water are not encouraging and have ended up in severely affecting the mass population world over including developed and developing countries. Thus, the need of the hour is heavy reliance and committed implementation of alternatives like water harvesting, watershed management, efficient water management system, appropriate water policy, transparent regulatory mechanism and effective water conservation. If above becomes reality then, "Do we need privatization of water?"

References

Agarwal, Anil, Narain, Sunita and Khurana, Indira (2001), "Making Water Everybody's Business: Practice and Policy of Water Harvesting", New Delhi: Centre for Science and Environment, www.cseindia.org.

Chakraborty, Sanghamitra (8 June, 2003), "Can Privatisation Plug India's Leaking Bucket?", *Times News* Network.

"Corruption, the Companion of Privatization", Public Services International Briefing World Water Forum, The Hague, 17–22 March, 2000.

"Degremont Water Plant Will Leave Tehri Farmers High and Dry", (July 15, 2002), *Business Line*.

Dhar, Aarti (12 April, 2003), "Chattisgarh to Cancel Water Supply Contract", *The Hindu*.

Ghotge, Sanjeev (October 2002), "India's Water Policy: A Perspective Paper", Pune, National Centre for Advocacy Studies.

Hall, David (July 1999), "Privatization, Multinationals and Corruption," Public Services International Research Unit, Report No. 9909-U-U-Corrup.doc.

http://studentorgs.utexas.edu/aidaustin/water/water_privatization.pdf. (Water Privatization and Implications in India Anitha Sampath, Balakrishnan Kedarnath, Chandrika Ramanujam, Hozefa Haidery, Rajesh Rao, Ravishankar Arunachalam, Sandhya Govindaraju, Vennila Thirumalavan, Vishv Jeet Association for India's Development).

http://www.atimes.com/atimes/South_Asia/.

http://www.infoforhealth.org, (Solutions for Water Short World), 2006.

"Integrated Watershed Management: Key to Sustaining SAT Productivity", Farmers' Training on Integrated Watershed Management, 7 February, 2001, ICRISAT, Patancheru, Andhra Pradesh, India, http://www.rainwaterharvesting.org.

Jain, Sonu (13 April, 2003), "A River Gone Private is Drying Up", *The Sunday (Indian) Express*.

Kamath, Anjali (28 May, 2002), "Water Profiteers", *Corp Watch India*.

Kaur, Naunidhi (30 August–12 September, 2003), "Privatising Water", *Frontline*, Vol. 20, Issue 18.

Lobina and Hall, "UK Water Privatisation: A Briefing", (PSIRU, February, 2001), Section 2.2.B, http://www.psiru.org/reports/2001–02-W-UK-over.doc.

Mehdudia, Sujay (29 November, 2000), "Sheila Dixit Plays Slander Campaign", *The Hindu*.

Mehta, Abhay (2000), *Power Play: A Study of the Enron Project*, Orient Longman Publishers.

National Water Policy (2002) for India at http://wrmin.nic.in/policy/nwp2002.

Nityanand, Jayaraman (28 May, 2002), "No Water? Drink Coke", *Corp Watch India*.

Report of The United Nations Department of Economic and Social Affairs (DESA), (2004), Division for Sustainable Development, Agenda 21, Chapter 18.

Sharma, Ashwani (14 July, 2002), "Water Colour of Money", *The Sunday (Indian) Express*.

Sharma, Reeta (20 January, 2001), "Anna Hazare: A Fearless Crusader", *The Tribune*.

Shiva, Vandana (2002), *Water Wars: Privatization, Pollution and Profit*, South End Press.

Shiva, Vandana (31 July, 2002), "Water Privatization in India", Article in Public Citizen Website.

Sridhar, Lalitha (7 June, 2006), Water: The Privatization Debate, India Resource Center, http://www.corpwatchindia.org/.

Too Much Too Little: The Characteristics of Water in India, Development Alternatives Website.

Top 10 Reasons to Oppose Water Privatization, Public Citizen Website.

"Water Privatization Fiascos: Broken Promises and Social Turmoil", Public Citizen Report.

World Commission on Dams, Dams and Development: A New Framework for Decision-Making, www.dams.org/report, especially Chapter 5, Thematic Review 4.3 and background papers on rainwater harvesting.

5 Sustainable Development in Agriculture

Role of Some Non-Government Organizations in Western Maharashtra

R.B. Patil

The Global Partnership for Environment and Development: A Guide to Agenda 21 of UNCED has given importance to the role of NGOs as these are considered as partners for sustainable development. It has stressed that the formidable global network of NGOs, operating at the international, national and local levels, should be tapped, enabled and strengthened.

Non-governmental organizations (NGOs) play a vital role in shaping and implementing participatory democracy. Independence is one of their major attributes and is the precondition of real participation. The credibility of NGOs lies in the responsible and constructive role they play in society. These organizations, including those non-profit organizations representing major social groups, possess well-established and diverse expertise in fields which will be of particular importance to the implementation and monitoring of environmentally sound, socially responsible and sustainable development.

Nearly seventy NGOs are working in Maharashtra for sustainable development in agriculture. The paper deals with some of the NGOs in Western Maharashtra.

Maharashtra Organic Farming Federation (MOFF), Pune

MOFF is a group of organizations and farmers involved in organic farming movement. MOFF is a registered public trust under Bombay Public Trust Act, 1960. MOFF consists of one/two persons from each district. It has affiliated model farms at each Taluka with some volunteer's organizations and farmers.

The process started after State-Level Workshop on Organic Farming organized by Gramparivartan—NGO and state agriculture department on 5 April, 2003. V.B. Foundation played a crucial role of coordinating with special invitees. Around 750 participants from government and NGOs participated in the workshop.

After this, Vikram Boke, Chairman of V.B. Foundation discussed with many organizations and farmers involved in organic farming. Then the concept of state level apex body emerged. V.B. Foundation organized a workshop on 26 July, 2003 at Pune which was attended by 66 organizations and farmers. The ad hoc body was established. V.B. Foundation participated in Kisan 2003 Exhibition in December 2003 and it received 47,000 letters and got more than 3,000 registrations for participation in MOFF.

Organic farming in the state received a shot in the arm when 15 successful organic farmers in various talukas opened their fields for 'study' to fellow farmers. The first farm in the series, developed by Tukaram Shitole at Nhavi Saandas in the Haveli taluka, was formally declared an 'organic (farming) school' by veteran Gandhian Balasaheb Bharde. The event was held, aptly, at the Gandhi Bhavan on 1st October, 2004 on the eve of Gandhi Jayanti. Organic farming is a key feature of the Gandhian ideal of a sustainable village. Sustainable agriculture is also the motto of the

MOFF, a statewide network of scientists, organic farmers and voluntary agencies.

Bokey said "the co-operative movement in the state has hit rock bottom, leaving farmers bankrupt. Successive governments have done them through promotion of wrong crop patterns, seeds, fertilizer overuse and over-irrigation. The cost of farming is growing without any rise in income. Multinationals like Monsanto are now set to rob the farmer of biodiversity. Organic farming is the answer to the loan-free farmer and pollution-free farming. The organic schools are actually farms on which organic farmers have successfully worked for the last three years or so. After all, seeing is believing. Every Sunday farmers from the taluka can visit the farm/school and experience the entire procedure. Organic farming does not merely mean the use of vermin-compost instead of chemical fertilizers: it is an entire system." (*Times of India*, 3 October 2004).

Gram Parivartan and Pani Panchayat, Pune

Both these organizations are working in the field of organic farming for sustainable development and distribution of water on equal justice.

Late Vilasrao Salunkhe has established Gramgourav Pratisthan in 1973 for rural development and Pani Panchayat is a social movement under it. The Naigaon Pattern has been successfully implemented for farmers cultivating jirait: non irrigated land. Smt. Kalpana Salunkhe has continued the work in the same direction.

Pandurang Shitole looks after the activities of Gram Parivartan which has been established in 1992. These two organizations jointly have formed a Study Team on Organic Farming. The report of the first meeting on 28th and 29th January, 2006 has been made available in which detailed discussion was held on the issue of land. Nearly 33 farmers practising organic farming and the experts attended the meeting.

Institute of Rural Credit and Entrepreneurship Development, Sangli

The institute has been registered under Bombay Public Trust Act of 1950. It has the main aim of food security for all. One of the programmes of the institute relates to agriculture.

Agriculture and Agri-Related Programmes

- Organic Farming Information and Promotion Centre.
- Farmer's Club.
- Agri-Produce Processing and Marketing, Land Development and Watershed Development.
- Vermi-Compost.
- Kitchen Garden.
- Promotion of Agri-Related Businesses, Grain Bank Programme (Production, Storage, Distribution and Marketing Management).
- Certification of Organic Farms.

The eastern part of Sangli district in Maharashtra state is remote, undulated, and drought-prone. Livelihood options are threatened by recurring risks of high credit rates, poor infrastructure facilities, and poor availability of seeds and lack of access to resources from government schemes. Due to effects of the "Green Revolution", increased use of chemical fertilizers and pesticides are sought to increase productivity. This has led to frustration and losses in the region largely resulting from the high expenditure, incurred on buying chemical fertilizers and pesticides, other than declining yields, improper information about usage and low rainfall. This has forced farmers to think of agriculture as a secondary occupation, leading to large-scale migration. Small farmers have been pushed into poverty and forced to work for rich farmers at low wages worsening their plight.

Project Goal

Promote organic farming in five chosen villages to demonstrate its ability to be sustainable as compared to high input farming being practised in neighbouring areas.

Project Details

A major aim of the project was to create awareness, and motivate the farmers to adopt indigenous organic farming techniques, leading to better profitability. This included addressing aspects of soil productivity by introducing various simple methods, i.e., vermi-composting, biodegradable farming waste, NADEP, organic compost, slurry making, etc. It also covered introduction of simple low cost farmer-friendly practises, i.e., green-manuring, seed priming-germination practises, supportive irrigation facilities like drip/pot irrigation, contour bunding, trenching and enhancing groundwater: water table recharge and conservation of soil loss.

Using farmer-friendly ways of working, the NGO conducted Participatory Rural Appraisals (PRAs), and initially took up vermi-composting with fifty farmers in five villages in Atapadi taluka of Sangli district. All 50 farmers harvested crops for two seasons, and have shared 1–2 kg earthworms with other farmers, free of cost as their contribution to further the programme. Since the project is ongoing, it has been reported that more than 100 farmers have taken up the programme, and this figure is going up with every passing season. The programme has extended to three more villages with farmers sharing results, and exchanging the methods to achieve them. More than eight farmers have taken to commercial production of vermi-composting and have collectively produced more than 7 metre of vermi-compost, that has been sold to the neighbouring farmers for a value more than Rs 1,25,000. Most farmers have adopted the techniques for the first time and are taking to producing compost round the year and its applicability has been extended to horticulture crops as well. They all feel that they have considerably lowered their cost of production that is now adding to their profits and improving their livelihood prospects.

Community Participation

The NGO approached the farmers through small informal kinship based groups. The communities looking for alternatives latched on the ideas and showed their greatness by not only sharing costs, taking decisions but also adopting technologies. Villagers further got the programme linked through village Panchayat.

Capacity Building Efforts

The NGO has done good work by helping dovetail the technique into efforts of government local bodies, Panchayats and agriculture departments. These bodies have been trained along with the community and more than 150 persons have been trained at different levels. The NGO has been approached by various government departments to function as a resource person and further the cause of vermi-composting. Many local publications have been printed and distributed. More than 10–12 local training sessions have been conducted and exposure trips organized. 'Learning-by-doing' has raised the confidence of farmers and demonstrated the firsthand benefits to others.

Observations

The period of gestation to switch over to organic cultivation can be a challenge that needs to be overcome and it will be useful to know how the same was addressed in this project. Over a period of time it will also be useful to understand if the organic produce is meant for self-consumption in a local area or meant to address needs of external markets that will then need many other aspects to be addressed. It has been recorded that some farmers have already shown the way to other villagers by selling their produce in a market-based system.

Learning from the Project

- The role of the NGO and its commitment to the project assume great importance as has been again demonstrated with this project. The fact that other villages are coming forth to take the programme further on their initiative adds conviction to the effort.

- One of the hindrances faced in the project region other than those resulting from natural causes and problems of staff management was that of distribution of free chemical fertilizer by a public sector entity. While many farmers refused to succumb to the temptation, it was difficult for others to do so. Given such a situation that may develop in the future, it will be good to strengthen the resolve of the beneficiaries and this can only be done if alternate livelihood options are in place to take care of economic needs in the short term and a state of heightened awareness is achieved.

Potential to Scale Up and Replicate Effort: A project such as this is highly suited for replication and scaling up given the inputs of the NGO and the level of activity that has been pursued by the project with a reasonable degree of success.

The Art of Living, Bangalore

Shri Shri Ravishankar established this foundation at Bangalore in 1980. The foundation has been spread in more than 142 countries of the world. The Art of Living has 5-H Programme action plan (Health, Hygiene, Homes, Human values, and Harmony in diversity).With reference to agriculture, the following activities are carried out:

Specific training programmes for farmers on the use of organic pesticides, fertilizers, and composting.

Encouraging the use of indigenous seeds over genetically modified seeds in order to maintain the natural biodiversity.

The establishment of cooperative seed storages so that the collection and distribution of seeds can be effectively done.

The 5-H Programme promotes soil and water conservation measures, tree plantation and the introduction of organic agriculture techniques, such as vermi-composting, and the use of natural pesticides, bio-fertilizers and effective micro-organisms. These measures contribute to enhanced crop growth and green manures. By encouraging organic systems of soil enrichment, soil and water conservation measures and the development of water resources, the cropping intensity on the land can be increased. Moreover, activities such as composting and vermin-composting provide additional income to the families and assist in the disposal of agricultural waste.

Almost 95 per cent of the village population is directly dependent on land for their livelihood; therefore agricultural improvement is of wide relevance to the villagers. The poorest farmers often own, or have access to limited tracts of land and so the priority for them is not only to improve individual crop yields, but also to increase overall land productivity, without increasing their dependence on chemicals such as fertilizers, pesticides, insecticides, etc., a dependency, which has led to increased indebtedness amongst farmers. Knowing no way out of their situation, close to 20,000 farmers have committed suicide in India during the 1994–1998 period.

In order to increase the outreach, the first Shri Shri Mobile Agriculture Institute (SSMAI) van was launched in October, 2003. The key objectives of the van are to provide guidance to farmers to become self-reliant and build up their inner confidence, to promote and revive organic farming, and to educate farmers on water management and irrigation. It also educates farmers in the use of quality agricultural inputs and implements aimed at higher quality yield among others. The promotion of chemical-free farming and awareness creation among the village population and particularly the farmers on biodiversity, the hazards of genetic engineering on the bio-safety, and the health hazards caused by the use of chemical products lie at the core of the interventions. SSMAI participates in local festivals (Kisan Melas) where it conducts exhibitions on agricultural activities, organizes educative film shows and establishes vermiculture units.

Apart from awareness creation, SSMAI conducts training on organic farming and Rishi Krishi, an ancient Vedic method of organic farming. Environmental conservation methods and optimum utilization of natural resources along with rainwater harvesting are also taught. In order to make its interventions more comprehensive, SSMAI distributes improved bullock drawing equipment, plant protection equipment, irrigation pipelines and sprinkler sets, some of them subsidized by the government.

At Phaltan in Satara district, the training camp was organized on 15th February, 2005 in the presence of Shri Shri Ravishankarji, Subhash Palekar gave guidance for zero budget natural farming.

An Overview

The Agenda 21 has given importance to the role of NGOs as these are considered partners for sustainable development. It has been observed that, alternative to High External Input Agriculture (HEIA), states, non-governmental organizations (NGOs) across the world are attempting to develop a framework—Low External Inputs and Sustainable Agriculture (LEISA)–for promoting Sustainable Agriculture Development (SAD). According to studies by M.A. Muttalib, and E.A. Brett, NGOs are preferred than state-owned machineries as the former provide effective and equitable services to the community (Rajendran).

In India, organic farming has to meet the dual challenges of sustaining the food productivity while causing minimum damage to the agro ecosystem and environment. Therefore, the challenges and constraints in adoption of organic farming on a wider scale in countries like India are quite unique.

The Agenda 21 stresses on strengthening the role of farmers. The report observes farmers in developing countries are often forced to overexploit their land, inevitably leading to the loss of soil fertility and lower crop yields. If agriculture is to meet future food demands in the decades ahead, farmers worldwide must be able to adopt practises that are both highly productive and sustainable. There are many NGOs working in all parts of Maharashtra in the field of organic farming. MOFF, Pune, Gram Parivartan, Pani Panchayat, Pune, Institute of Rural Credit and Entrepreneurship

Development, Sangli, and the Art of Living, are some of the NGOs working in Western Maharashtra who are performing significant role in sustainable development in agriculture.

References

Brett, E.A. (1993), "Voluntary Agencies as Development Organizations: Theorising the Problem of Efficiency and Accountability", *Development and Change*, 24(2), 269–303.

Muttalib, M.A. (1987), "Voluntarism and Development: Theoretical Perspectives", *The Indian Journal of Public Administration*, XXIII (3), 399–419.

News item: "Organic Farmers to Teach Success Story to Others: 50 Fields to Double Up as Sunday Schools", *The Times of India*, 3rd October, 2004.

Rajendran, S., "Non-governmental Organizations and Sustainable Agriculture Development in India".

UNCED, The Global Partnership for Environment and Development: A Guide to Agenda 21, 1992.

United Development Programme: 50 Global Environment Facility (GEF), Project Experiences.

6 Natural Resource Management and Development

S. Jeevananda Reddy

Natural resources/environment is the major casualty in almost all developmental activities—The two natural resources that are of importance are land and water. Because of this one cannot say that we do not need any developmental activities. The developmental activities must be sustainable in terms of management of natural resources on long term. The developmental activities could be classified as activities that benefit few people and the activities that benefit majority of the people. Irrigation projects, which are opposed by politicians to serve their political interests, come under the later group and the activities that are undertaken around Hyderabad, not opposed by politicians as wealth is coming to their doorsteps, come under the former group. The discussion in this article relates to developmental activities undertaken by government agencies that benefit few and cause environmental destruction and human miseries. Let us present few case studies of this nature in which we participated.

Urban Land: A Commodity

The urban land is simply regarded as a commodity and not as part of a large continuum, intimately linked to the surrounding air, water, vegetation and life, inflicting environmental/ecological damage. The latest Hyderabad Urban Development Authority (HUDA) auction of prime land of 23,500 sq metre adjoining KBRN Park at Jubilee Hills Checkpost is a classical example of this nature. It violates G.O. Ms. No. 423 and G.O., No. 86 of 3 March, 2006 giving free hand to the builders. In fact due to the intervention of environmental groups in the past, TDP government withdrew the allotment of this land to tourism department to build a seven-star hotel.

On the one hand, the government says that the outer ring road is being developed to ease the congestion in the Hyderabad metropolitan area and on the other hand it violates it own orders/government orders, permit development of congestion at Jubilee Hills Checkpost, which is already in trouble, through relaxation of the rules in favour of a private investor and endangering KBRN Park on a long-term.

To achieve the goals in the spirit of ecologically sustainable development, HUDA must first draft and approve the master plan by constituting Metropolitan Planning Committee as per Article 243-ZE of the Constitution of India with the future population zonal regulations and accordingly the building regulations should be subordinate to the approved master plan. In 1975, the Municipal Corporation of Hyderabad (MCH) notified a master plan by the name Development Plan under the MCH Act. Naturally, the plan was enforceable only to the extent of MCH area, which is around 172.60 sq km. The MCH area occupies around 9 per cent of the jurisdiction of HUDA (1,864.67 sq km). In 1975, no other municipality existed in HUDA area. HUDA was constituted in 1975 and in 1980 notified a master plan for the rest of metropolitan area (1,692.27 sq km). In 1994, HUDA prepared revised master plan with the target population of 2011. This is only a draft master plan. Draft master plans of 2020 were prepared with population projections of 2020/2021 in 2001. This is also a draft but the drafts are serving to manipulate and acquire lands of commercial value at important places by people in power and their families on their names and on their family members' names or benami names to amass wealth. A glaring example to this observation is that HUDA says it will finalize the draft master plan of 2020 after finalizing the outer ring road—master plan development has become a mafia planning (and thus HUDA became a real estate mafia centre) instead of scientific planning to solve and meet the needs of projected population. That is, land is being used as a commodity!

Destruction of Water Bodies

Mohd. Quli Qutub Shaw on the banks of Musi River founded Hyderabad in 1591. The city has a glorious tradition of lakes and gardens built by the rulers—Qutub Shaw dynasty during 1564–1724 AD and Asaf Jahi dynasty during 1724–1948 AD. The Hyderabad District Water Conservation Committee with the help of NRSA, identified 932 tanks in HUDA area covering 22,623.31 ha. Of these, tanks with more than 10 ha. are 173 with area occupied by 20,592 ha. HUDA on 4 May, 2000 identified 169 tanks/lakes with more than 10 ha. and issued a notification stating that "The entire area, falling within the full tank level of the lakes as per the Survey of India Maps, must be kept free from any types of constructions irrespective of ownership or any land use or master/zonal development plans that may have been previously notified. In addition, a buffer belt of 30 metre within on all sides of each lake must be kept free from any type of construction in the interest of prevention of pollution to the lake waters and allow free flow of water to the lakes". Though through this notification HUDA has done a marvellous job but it failed in protecting them, as they were not demarcated to date. Government departments intend to do a good job bringing out government orders/notifications but they rarely implement them, even after High Court/Supreme Court directing them to do so. With this, in the last five-year period, majority of these lakes/tanks are and are being either encroached or polluted. Let me give the destructions meted to three important lakes that served the drinking water needs of the twin cities in the past and at present, namely Himayatsagar, Osmansagar and Hussainsagar lakes along with river Musi.

Himayatsagar and Osmansagar Lakes

On the advise of Sir M. Visvesvaraya, the legendary engineer of India, Himayatsagar and Osmansagar lakes were built on Musi and its tributary Easi to contain floods after severe floods in September 1908. Osmansagar lake was built in the year 1913 and Himayatsagar lake was built in 1927. Since around 1930 started using the water from these two lakes for drinking purposes in addition to agriculture purposes. These two lakes have a supply capacity of around 85 MCM (45 MGD), which was just sufficient for the population of 1.25 million (it is the population of 1961)—this is more or less freely available. These two lakes also recharge the dwindling groundwater. At present, both these lakes are providing 27 MGD of water directly and around the same amount indirectly through groundwater in this zone.

The government noticed reduction in water flow and contamination of water with the growth of population and associated construction activities to meet their needs as well as use of chemical fertilizers and pesticides in agriculture with the green revolution technology in the catchment areas of the two lakes. Though Water Act of 1974 and Air Act of 1981 and Environment Act of 1986 are there to protect water bodies, the state government of Andhra Pradesh felt these are not adequate and to have preventive measures, felt the need to apply 'precautionary principle' and took special steps and issued G.O. Ms. No. 50 MA, 18 January, 1989 prohibiting construction of building works/check dams/lift irrigation works/storage reservoirs across streams flowing in the catchment areas of these two lakes. Also prohibited use in agriculture of chemical fertilizers and pesticides/insecticides that contaminate surface and groundwater. Subsequently, the government noticed new problems affecting the quality of water in the two lakes. The Hyderabad Metropolitan Water Supply and Sewerage Board appointed a technical committee to look into this issue and suggest ways and means of controlling these so that water of the two lakes can be protected from contamination as well as contain the reduction of water flow into these two lakes. Based on the first interim report of the committee the government issued G.O. Ms. No. 192 MA, 31 March, 1994. Subsequently after receiving the second interim report of the committee the G.O. 192 was modified and issued G.O. Ms. No. 111 of 8 March, 1996. Thus, it is to be seen that G.O. Ms. No. 192 and 111 were passed by the government of Andhra Pradesh as per the recommendations made by experts to preserve the quantity and quality of water in Himayatsagar and Osmansagar lakes which supply drinking water. The G.O. 50 of 1989 is part of G.O. 111 of 1996. The G.O. 111 order says that:

> (i) To prohibit polluting industries, major hotels, residential colonies or other establishments that generate pollution in the catchment of the lakes upto 10 km from full tank level of the lakes as per list in Annexure-I (Annexure-I contains 84 villages falling within the 10 km). However, residential developments in residential use zone may be permitted. The following measures shall be taken to protect water flowing into the lakes: (a) 60 per cent of the total area shall be kept as open space and roads in all layouts in the villages of catchment area; (b) The land use of about 90 per cent of the area is classified as recreational and conservation use in the master plan. The Hyderabad Urban Development Authority should take action for the classification of the 90 per cent of the area as agriculture, which is inclusive of horticulture and floriculture; (c) To restrict the FSI to 1:0.5 in the catchment area. This measure will ensure that 90 per cent of the area remains under agriculture, as is the practice now and ensure protection of the lakes; (d) To prohibit polluting industries within 10 km radius (i.e., both on upstream and downstream side of the lakes) to prevent acidification of lakes due to air pollution; (e) There shall be total prohibition of location of industries in the prohibited zone, etc.

Contrary to this government order, TDP government permitted Surana Industry, a pollution potential industry, within the 10 km radius by granting exemption. On this, Justice Jaganadha Rao (Hon'ble Supreme Court) upheld the government order and passed orders along with cancelling the orders issued to Surana Industry by the state government as "The State of Andhra Pradesh is therefore directed hereby to identify these industries located within 10 km radius of these two lakes and to take action in consultation with APPCB to prevent pollution of the drinking water in these two reservoirs. The State and the Board shall not permit any polluting industries within the 10 km radius. In our view, the Environmental (Protection) Act, 1986 and the Water Act, 1974 and the Air Act, 1981 have enough provisions applicable not only to new industries proposed to be established but also to existing industries". With this order two things are clear that (a) upstream, downstream and 84 villages are replaced by 10 km radius from the FTL and (b) according to Environmental Act, industry can be any operation or process. After taking into account all these aspects, APPCB has prepared a map with the help of remote sensing demarcating the 10 km radius around the two lakes. Accordingly some of the polluting industries/activities were closed and some were shifted and some are being shifted. No new industry/activity that has the pollution potential was given permission—the consent was rejected to a potato chips factory by an NRI, CDFD by a central government institute, golf course by an NRI near Gandipet, Pragati Resorts, etc. While rejecting wet operations in the case of CDFD, APPCB authorities have duly taken into consideration along with other things, the opinion given by the Advocate General, which shows "In the case of area within the 10 km there is an absolute ban on polluting activity. The wording of G.O. Ms. No. 111 is very simple and plain. All establishments that generate pollution in the catchment area upto 10 km are banned".

The 'spirit' of all these sequence of government orders and orders is "to prohibit activities that affect quality and quantity of water flowing into the lakes". The primary responsibility of the government in general and government departments in specific shall be to interpret 'more stringently' the G.O. 111 in this direction and safeguard the drinking water in the two lakes and not to put holes into G.O. 111 to serve the 'vested interests' thereby causing damage to these two lakes. As per the G.O. 111, there is no clause to permit the change of land use in the prohibited zone.

Kill crows and feed eagles: By closing the existing industries and not permitting new industries coming up in the 10 km radius zone of the two lakes and allowing more hazardous activities like airport, resorts, golf courses, cottages, townships, commercial activities, etc., that generate not only the domestic sewage that contains toxic chemicals but also use of chemical fertilizers and pesticides in the development of greenbelts/lawns, etc., is more catastrophic to these two water bodies. The Hon'ble Supreme Court (judgment, 1 December 2000) in its order says that "In fact, exemption granted even to a single major hazardous industry might itself be sufficient to make the water in the reservoirs totally unsafe for drinking purposes—Such an order of exemption carelessly passed, ignoring the 'precautionary principle' could be catastrophic". Precautionary principle means 'prevention measures' rather than 'control measures'.

In violation of all these, the two notorious government departments, namely HUDA and Tourism—bent upon destroying these two water bodies to serve vested interests. The argument is: we can bring Krishna water by depriving drinking and irrigation needs of drought-prone Rayalaseema and Telangana instead of protecting freely available water resources. Let me present few such cases:

Shamshabad International Airport

Even after the Supreme Court judgment (1 December 2000) with reference to Surana Industry, TDP government gave permission to establish an international airport at Shamshabad, which is a highly polluting activity in the prohibited zone. On this, environmental groups approached the High Court. The proponent agreed to shift all polluting activities including hotels outside 10 km radius of 10 km the FTL of the two lakes. Yet there remain one and half runways and terminal building in the prohibited zone. The proponent submitted that the water collected in this zone will be taken to ETP that will be constructed outside the 10 km radius for the treatment of wastewater. With this, no authority can stop other commercial and residential activities around it that cause severe pollution to lakes and restrict the water flow into the lakes. The fact is, politicians/bureaucrats acquired huge acres of land around the proposed airport and with this the airport was not taken outside the prohibited area. In fact, during Y.S. Rajashekara Reddy's, the Chief Minister of the state's visit to this area under first chief minister Rajiv 'palle bata' programme the realtors asked the chief minister to relax G.O. 111 and on this environmentalists sent their protests to chief minister. Chief minister asked the EPTRI to study the whole issue. EPTRI in its report brought out the illegal activities in violation of government orders and causing pollution along with the checkdams that were permitted by TDP government in violation of government orders. The report recommended implementing the government orders more stringently. So far the government has not initiated any action on these illegal activities in violation of G.O. 111.

Outer Ring Road (ORR) Phase-I

It is the second step of Shamshabad airport, a classical example for setting the stage for the destruction of the two lakes. Though Outer Ring Road-I (ORR-I) is to help in the decongestion of the MCH area, instead it is being built to serve the bada babu's commercial/anti-social activities in the prohibited zone only. When HUDA sought our response on the ORR-Phase-I, we clearly told them that this alignment violates the G.O. 111 and Supreme Court order and suggested instead to construct overbridge on the existing inner ring road from Gachibowli—Mehadipatnam—Samshabad (now the government has taken up this project from Mehdipatnam to Aram Ghar), so that we can protect the two water bodies as well there is no need to acquire additional land for this purpose. Even with 100 per cent opposition to ORR Phase-I alignment at the public hearing they went ahead to benefit the bigwigs who hold huge chunks of land in the prohibited area of 10 km radius of two lakes to develop commercial activity—the unscientific approach of ORR alignment was exposed by the media the HUDA's unscientific deals. HUDA is also planning to complete the destruction of the two lakes by their unscientific deals: (a) building luxury villas for NRIs on 200–300 acre of land at Budvel overlooking Himayatsagar lake on a hill top (*The Times of India* reports, 10 and 11 May 2006); (b) alienation of 33 acre of land at Vatti Nagulapalli village in favour of IAS officers, judges, MPs, MLAs and media personnel (*The Times of India*, 16 May, 2006)—this allocation of land to all powerful group in the banned area clearly shows the thinking of the government to destroy these two lakes, etc. In fact, HUDA while getting clearance from APPCB informed the committee that there will be no commercial activities along the ORR-I and agreed to develop 500 metre green belt/plantations between ORR-I and edge of Himayatsagar lake bund and intersections will be permitted at state and national highways (but now decided to have intersections at every 8 km). The whole buzz of commercial activity got limelight with the auction of 100 acre at Kokapet in the prohibited zone for Rs 10–15 crore per acre. When the environmental groups raised the issue of G.O. 111 and Supreme Court order, HUDA issued statements saying that they issued the government order and therefore they are the right persons to interpret the government order. After all this halla-gulla HUDA decided to amend the government order to suit the vested interests by throwing the Supreme Court order in dustbin. None of the political parties raised the issue of environment as most of them have their own vested interests in these deals.

The *New Indian Express* report in 25 June, 2005 issue states that on one side by spending crores of rupees HUDA is developing urban forestry and destroying reserve forests and on the other to serve the vested interests against all rules/laws, government orders, Supreme Court orders—and ORR-I pass very close to Mrugavani National Park in violation of Rule 35, Sub-Rule 5 and Rule 20 of the Wildlife (Protection) Act, 1972 including Amendment Act 2002; judgment of Hon'ble Supreme Court of India dated 30 October, 2002 regarding any encroachments into reserve forests and forest lands; MOE and Notification No. S.O. 891(E) 4th August, 2003, etc. To serve the needs of vested interests HUDA changed the alignment (APPCB rejected the original alignment drawn to serve the vested interests and approved an alignment that is not going to effect the Chilukuri Reserve Forest, Mrugavani National Park and Himayatsagar but after a month again got the original plan approved).

Hussainsagar Lake and Musi River

Hussainsagar Lake

Built in 1562 AD, with a magnificent stretch of 20.7 sq km is a treasure and heritage water body of Hyderabad and it falls within the limits of Hyderabad Urban Development Authority (HUDA). It has been an ecological asset of the twin cities, as its water spread has not only kept the climate of the city in equilibrium but also helped water table recharge in the areas around it. The first source of water supply to Hyderabad was from Hussainsagar lake. The water of Hussainsagar was sufficient for the people of Hyderabad around 1891. The water of the lake served the drinking water needs till around 1930. This also protected the citizens living in low-lying areas around the lake from imminent threat from floods. Various encroachments have been taking place in and around the lake over the past 30 years or so, like encroachments by slum dwellers, rich real estate groups and the government agencies have reduced the lake area by around 60 per cent. It was further reduced by way of roads, artificial amusement parks, sewage treatment plant, residential buildings, etc. The catchment area has been neglected and effluents of different types polluted the inflows into the lake—domestic sewage and industrial effluents. The industrial pollution found its way into the lake since 1964. The immersion of Ganesh idols that were made of toxic paints and non-biodegradable materials/plaster of paris, iron, etc., have further added to the pollution of the lake. In the past several years, several concerned citizens and environmental groups are fighting against this menace.

Around 115 mld of sewage is reaching Hussainsagar lake and of which only about 20 mld is treated to date (?) and released into the lake along with around 30 mld untreated effluents (?) and the rest is bypassed. By treating the majority of the effluents, they will serve the needs of gardening of surrounding areas/gardens/parks as well increase the water table recharge capacity of the lake at the same time improve the aesthetic picture around the lake. Unfortunately this was not undertaken but on the contrary the water is let out from the lake and then encroachment of the lake by filling the lake bed with the soil with tacit support from government agencies!

Government built the Necklace Road in 1996 to indicate this boundary of the lake—supposed to be developed as the green belt between the lake and Necklace Road. Yet it has continued to fill up the lake areas and to convert the reclaimed areas into centres of commercial activities and a concrete jungle, violating the rules and regulations in the name of tourism/eco-tourism in and around notified areas of Hussainsagar lake. According to the 4th May, 2000 notification of HUDA, the Hussainsagar lake area is shown as 549.23 ha. equivalent to 1,356 acre, but HUDA presented on 11th November, 2003 at a public consultation workshop on "Restoration and Management of Hussainsagar Waters" as 1,066 acre—reduced by 290 acre. Through the illegal actions of HUDA, the lake area have been continuously reduced and thus the present area may be far lower than 1,066 acre—though through the G.O. Ms. No. 575 MA, 12 December, 2000 (after the HUDA notification of 4 May, 2000) the government has established Buddha Purnima Project Authority. Yet, unfortunately, to make it easy to violate rules and regulations, Hussainsagar lake is put under the control of several government organs, such as HUDA, Buddha Purnima Project Authority, MCH, Tourism Department, Irrigation Department, etc. The vested interests manipulated the authorities and got access to prime land around the lake to develop commercial places.

With all these, HUDA is looking for a soft loan of Rs 250 crore from Japan under the disguise of beautification of the lake, to develop more commercial activities in and around the lake. Now the Necklace Road surroundings have become a hot bed for anti-social activities like prostitution and drugs. Though the Hon'ble High Court has given certain directions, with reference to PILs to the concerned government agencies/organizations, things are moving as usual around Hussainsagar lake. Writ Petition No. 23,768 of 2000, judgment delivered on 15 June, 2001: the operative part of the judgment is: (a) No further permanent structures including those involving commercial activities may be allowed to be raised on or near the water spread or catchment area; and (b) it also directed that the construction of an amusement park etc., may be allowed subject to examination and certification by AP Pollution Control Board that creation of such entertainment parks etc., would result only in sustainable development and would not create any ecological imbalance. Supreme Court appointed a three-member committee to look into the whole gambit of Hussainsagar lake and submit the report. The committee submitted its report but the court has not found time to deliver the judgment! In the case of Ganesh immersion several High Court order/government orders are there but the government departments are sleeping on these reports/orders/government orders. Now Hon'ble High Court first ordered no immersion from this year but later amended saying from next year. The final judgment has yet to be delivered!

With loan from Japan the government is planning to upgrade the 20 mld STP to tertiary and two more new STPs of 15 mlds each are planned. But, the government has not taken any steps to contain industrial effluents entering into sewage lines. Without this there is no way STP can treat industrial effluents. Government agencies are not committed in protection of the lake.

Musi River

With the rapid growth in urban centres the waste water generated is directly proportional to population growth. According to 2001 Census, the capital city has a population of 57.5 lakh, which was 4.5 lakh in 1901. That is, around 10 lakh families are living in the capital city in 2001—this may be doubled by 2020. The water supply by the Metro Water Board is around 215 MGD. In addition, people use an equal amount of underground water (bore wells) to meet their daily requirements. Of this around 80 per cent takes the shape of waste water, wherein only less than 10 per cent of this is treated presently. Thus, around 1,500 mld is left to enter water bodies and Musi everyday—this will increase with the increased population/activities in proportion in future. That means majority of this (bore well) enters the River Musi daily en route polluting groundwater, lakes, vagus, nallahs, drains, etc. In addition to the sewage, the runoff from the rainfall also follows the same route and with this pollution is carried to a long distance even in Musi river.

The sewage treatment plant (STP) at Amberpet receives 275 mld of sewer waste water, which includes 2 mld of industrial effluents from Common Effluent Treatment Plant at Jeedimetla and 7 mld of untreated and partially treated effluents from the neighbouring industries joining Musi directly. Of this 115 mld is partially treated and discharged into the River Musi along with the balance of 160 mld, which is bypassed directly into the River Musi without any treatment. The samples at the inlet and outlet of Amberpet STP (samples of 19th October, 2000) indicate respectively COD–553 and 267 mg/L, BOD–375 and 168 mg/L, not meeting the standards. Also, the effective operation of STP appears to be very very poor.

The observations carried out along the River Musi at 5 observational sites during May to August, 2001 indicate above standard limits in several parameters. The spread of PH, TDS, chlorides, sulphates, etc. are around the same along the course of the river, indicating the problem of pollution is not only confined to where the pollutants are joining the River Musi but also spread all along the downstream. In the case of nitrates and phosphates, they are high at the point of pollutants joining the river in dry season but this polluting effect increases after rains.

Industrial Effluents: Industrial areas have been developed in Musi basin after 1960. Major percentage of industries in these industrial areas consists of synthetic organic chemicals (bulk drugs and intermediates), lead extraction units, oil refineries, textiles, tanneries, electroplating units and distilleries. There are about 182 industries discharging their untreated/partially treated/treated effluents directly/indirectly into River Musi. The majority of these industries are located in the Sanathnagar, Chandulal Baradari, Azamabad, Bhahadurpura, Chandrayanagutta, Musheerabad, Kattedan, Uppal, Nacharam, LB Nagar, Hayatnagar, Jeedimetla and Balanagar industrial estates. In addition to these legally operating units there are several illegal units operating in this belt. There are three common effluent treatment plants (JETL, Jeedimetla and IDPL, Balanagar; PETL, Patancheru) functioning in this zone.

At present, untreated and undertreated industrial effluents from various industrial estates and the industries in unorganized sector in and around Hyderabad are finding their way into Musi river through open drains, pipelines, sewers etc. The STPs, which are basically capable of treating predominantly degradable organic wastes like domestic sewage, will not be able to treat the toxic industrial effluents, except diluting them, without reducing the total pollution load being discharged into Musi river. Some of the main sources are:

Katedan Industrial Estate discharges toxic effluents into Noor Mohd Kunta, (Katedan lake), which find their way into Musi river through Miralam tank. The efforts are being made by APPCB for the last couple of years, as per the directions of AP High Court and Supreme Court of India, have not yielded any results in preventing these discharges. The Supreme Court Monitoring Committee (SCMC) for Hazardous Wastes, vide its letter 12 February, 2005, directed the state government and APPCB to submit a time-bound proposal for rehabilitation of Katedan lake. The National Geophysical Research Institute (NGRI) results of Katedan industrial belt in the Musi river basin indicate high levels of arsenic in the soil in surrounding areas which ranges from 8 to 15 ppm with a limit of 2 ppm, lead of more than 1000 ppm with a limit of 50 ppm, and water samples revealed high levels of lead, strontium (2000 ppb with limit of 100 ppb) and selenium (of more than 20 ppb with a limit of 10 ppb) in the area. All these are hazardous for human health as they can enter the human body through food and water chain.

Common Effluent Treatment Plant, Jeedimetla (JETL) is discharging undertreated industrial effluents, which do not conform to the norms stipulated by CPCB, into duplicate K-S mains of municipal sewers, ultimately finding their way into Musi river through Amberpet STP. The SCMC also directed CETPs to ensure that their effluents meet the standard of reusable waters and the discharges into the public environment, including rivers is suspended within a time bound period. Final treated effluents of Jeedimetla CETP at V-notch before joining sewer observed during different periods of 2000 indicated phenol of 37 to 66.4 mg/L (limit 5 mg/L); ammonical nitrogen 167 mg/L (limit 50 mg/L), iron of 0.53 to 3.95 mg/L; lead of 0.34 to 0.63 mg/L (limit 0.1 mg/L); etc. It is the case with IDPL, Balanagar treatment plant. Common Effluent Treatment Plant, Pattancheru (PETL) is laying 18 km pipeline to transfer its undertreated industrial effluents, which do not conform to norms stipulated by CPCB, into municipal sewers, which again find their way into Musi river through Amberpet STP. The SCMC directed that PETL plant is restrained from transferring its effluents through 18 Km pipeline to Amberpet STP. It is nothing but shifting the problem from Nakka Vagu to Musi river. That means around 350 tons of toxic and non-degradable substances are let out into Musi river every day.

During non-rainy season (October to June) almost all these substances find their way into surface and groundwater (bore well) and the soil within 10 to 40 km of Amberpet STP, where the effluent waters are being utilized for agriculture, fish ponds, etc. This severely effects the health of human, animal and plant life. The groundwater in Patancheru area indicates arsenic levels upto 700 ppb (limit 10 ppb) from industries; and Hyderabad urban areas indicate nitrate of 1.2 to 760 mg/L (limit 45 mg/L) from urban sewage and copper of 0.03 to 0.49 mg/L (limit (0.05 mg/L) from industries; and Osmansagar area indicates sulphates of 673 to 1996 mg/L (limit 200 mg/L) from agriculture.

The unorganized sources like electroplating units, battery reconditioning units, vehicle repair workshops, metal fabrication units, painting workshops, several small scale industries working in the residential zones, etc., are discharging untreated effluents which find its way into Musi river through open drains.

What needs to be taken into account is not the volume of effluents and concentration levels of pollutants but the Total Maximum Daily Load (TDML) and the characteristics of various non-degradable, toxic and persistent bio-accumulative pollutants such as TDS, heavy metals, POPs etc., that are being discharged into the River Musi or any water body. The dilution factor does not help bringing down the TDML of the above stated pollutants, except reducing their concentration levels. Simple upgradation of STP is not going to help in bringing down TDML that is going to be added to the river Musi. Therefore, what matters to the villages downstream is the load, as wastewater is used for agricultural purposes and fish tanks. Any further discharge of TDML into Musi, which is already estimated to be receiving more than 400 tons TDS per day will only aggravate the alarming situation that already exists in the villages downstream of Musi.

The government has initiated 'Save Musi Project' at a cost of around Rs 900 crore. For this purpose, entire Musi stretch in the city has been divided into three zones—Tippu Khan bridge-Puranapul (ecological precinct), Puranapul-Chaderghat bridge area (heritage precinct) and Chaderghat bridge-Nagole (metropolitan precinct). In the heritage precinct it is planned to construct checkdams. Sewage enters the Musi from 18 sewer lines from different parts of the city. The sewage from these sewers are collected at five points where STPs are built: at Amberpet (339 mld), at Nagole (172 mld), at Nallacherivu (30 mld), at Zia Guda and at Nandimurisalai (Attapur 51 mld). The basic objective of the 'Save Musi Campaign' can be achieved only when the effluents (treated, untreated, partially treated) from industries and three CETPs is stopped from entering sewer lines/Musi along with cleansing of Musi bed from toxic contaminants. Also, there is no way with new building regulations to stop domestic sewage entering the Musi from upstream of the present project area. There is one another important issue is the running of STPs effectively all the time. All these contribute to severe odour problem by storing water through checkdams in the heritage precinct.

Also, bringing all the sewage to STPs erected along Musi river is not the correct approach. The STPs must be located at different places in the city and the treated wastewater can be used to fill the local tanks that will facilitate groundwater (bore well) recharge to meet the growing water needs of different parts of the city.

Nagarjunasagar Reservoir

The whole exercise of uranium mining is to keep the jobs of the employees engaged in this activity intact and share the spoils of contacts along with political leaders through contracts to the tune of hundreds and thousands of crore of the public money. The main problem with the Nalgonda uranium mining and processing is the contamination of Nagarjunasagar reservoir water that is going to effect 2–3 crore population in six districts through irrigation/food production and drinking water. It is also going to affect the population in twin cities of Hyderabad-Secunderabad who drink this water. The whole argument of the proponents of uranium mining revolves round the nuclear power production using uranium.

How essential is the nuclear power with uranium as fuel? In 2001, NEDCAP organized a National Renewable Energy Convention in Hyderabad. The then Minister of State for

Non-conventional Energy Sources, Government of India, Mr. M. Kannappan in his inaugural address stated that (a) "According to estimates prepared by the Ministry of Non-conventional Energy Sources there is a potential for generating upto 45,000 MW from wind energy, 15,000 MW from small hydro power projects and 19,500 MW from biomass sources. There is also potential for the installation of 12 million biogas plants and 140 million sq metre of solar thermal collectors" and (b) "The Prime Minister has already announced that 10,000 MW of power generating capacity will be added from renewable energy sources by the year 2012. This constitutes 10 per cent of the projected new generation capacity of 1,00,000 MW to be installed from all sources by 2012". In addition to these, there is a potential to save energy around 25 per cent of the total production and by including reduction in transmission losses it will be around 40 to 45 per cent of the total production.

Energy saved is also energy produced. At that time energy produced from all sources is one lakh MW and by 2012 it is expected to be two lakh MW and 40 to 45 per cent means 80,000 to 90,000 MW. The total potential of nuclear power from uranium is a meagre 10,000 to 20,000 MW after lakhs of crores of public money spending and causing human and environmental misery—with non-conventional energy sources alone the potential is 1,00,000 MW. Is this what the public wanted? Some argue that huge quantities of uranium are being produced by Canada and Australia. Why not we? Japan and France meeting their power needs through nuclear power. Why not we? Canada and Australia have vast area compared to India on the one hand and the mining is carried by private investors under the strict government acts. In India, we are not able to control pollution from a single industry even adjacent to capital city Hyderabad—most of the tanks and groundwater in almost all the industrial estates are polluted—what is the fate with the government agencies with very poor track record in pollution control? After Three-mile Island incident (Chernobyl incident in Russia) America decided in 1978 not to have any more nuclear power reactors. Germany, Sweden, Belgium, etc., decided not to go for nuclear power. Germany is effectively utilizing solar energy to meet its power needs. We can see Tirumala/TTD as-an example of effective utilization of wind power and solar power. The cost of production of non-conventional and conventional energy is Re 1 per unit then to produce the same one unit of nuclear power costs around Rs 1,000 (including present and future costs—fuel production, fuel production from uranium, maintenance of all types of wastes from mining to uranium/fuel processing, dismantling of nuclear power plant after its lifetime of 25–30 years). Is it the right approach for a country like India to produce nuclear energy at huge costs that creates environmental and human hazards. Though APPCB and water board rejected this project, the proponents are hell bent to go ahead with the mining and process not only in Nalgonda district but also at Kadapa district. These projects have around 1,600 crore to share through contracts! Should we put 2–3 crore population at danger to produce a meagre nuclear power at exorbitant cost?

Conclusions

The major casualty of ad hoc/unplanned/un-scientific developmental activities is in general the natural resources and in specific water bodies. This is quite significantly seen in Andhra Pradesh in general and in Hyderabad in specific. The major beneficiaries are the politicians, bureaucrats and realtors. In this whole process, scientific community is least bothered as it is more worried about its salaries, promotions and postings.

7 Role Assigned to Women by Development Advocates

Implications to Gender Equity

Swarna S. Vepa

It was felt that women's welfare remains neglected unless special efforts are made to include them in development programmes. Since the economic growth and development per se would not be gender sensitive, it is advocated that conscious effort will have to be made to draw as many women as possible into the development programmes. It was feared that women may be excluded from enjoying the fruits of development, such as opportunities of education, opportunities of employment and access to resources, if they are not made part of development process and programmes. It has been argued that gender sensitive development planning is important to take care of women's welfare as the beneficiaries of development.

It is further argued that women's special practical needs and their strategic needs get neglected if the development programmes are not made gender sensitive. Special needs address requirement for maternity leave, facilities for working mothers, laws prohibiting the employees to make women work late hours and so on. Women's strategic needs include needs women identify as crucial to achieve gender equity and gender justice. Equal pay for equal work, removal of discrimination in hiring for supervisory positions, right to land ownership, rights of inheritance and so on are some of the strategic needs of women. Women's equality is often seen as being associated with labour force participation, independent wage income, participation in public activity outside the home, less male-dominated property rights regime, decision-making at home and so on.

The views on women and development have undergone change over a period. First, women were recognized as the beneficiaries of development and the effort was made to include them in plans and programmes that benefited women. Women were basically recipients of development. Later, the importance of women as agents of development has been recognized. Though the word 'Women's agency' has been coined by Prof. Amartya Sen, more recently, their role as agents of change has been recognized long before. It is found for example that mother's education has an impact of declining infant mortality rate, fewer school dropouts, and better health care for the family. Many studies have shown that women's work participation and education reduced the fertility rates. As evidence piled up on these issues, women are recognized as active agents of change and dynamic promoters of social transformation that alter the lives of men and women.[1] The concept of women's participation in development gained credence. Participation of women in political, social and economic life outside the home is believed to bring about social change and contribute to the process of development.[2]

Further, as the women's organizations the world over gained voice, the women are sought to be recognized not as mere consumers of national income, and recipients of welfare measures, but contributors to national income. There is considerable controversy about women's unpaid work. Women perform a number of tasks related to the family business, related to household daily needs, in addition to cooking, cleaning and rearing children and caring for the elderly. The activities such as feeding the cattle, milking the cattle, cutting the fodder, tendering the vegetable garden and so on come under the category of work of family enterprise. Other activities such as fetching water, collecting fuel wood, wild foods, etc., add to the family income in kind. Taking care of the sick and the aged, looking after the children in addition to cooking and cleaning are also the responsibility of women.

The International System of National Accounting, popularly known as SNA included the value of production and services on one's own enterprise such as subsistence farm. However, women's activities within the household that contribute to the household enterprise have been excluded from the SNA for a long time. More recently women's contribution to household enterprise has been included. Some of the activities such as fetching water, collection of fuel wood, wild foods on one hand and caring for the sick and the aged on the other have been included as extended SNA activities. Very little information is available on the value of contribution to extended SNA by women. Only information available is[3] the time spent by women and men in six states on these activities.

It is true that household work and voluntary work of men and women is excluded from SNA. However, it remains a fact that some of the household work that contributes to the household income as well as community voluntary work that contributes to the national income are predominantly performed by women and their contribution is neglected. Thus, the role of women as contributors to national income has yet to be fully recognized. The reason why women's work is not fully recognized and included in the SNA, even by the United Nations is the fear that these large numbers of women may have to be brought under the labour protection laws by the governments.

Women's groups argued that the reproductive roles and child care responsibilities of women made work participation discontinuous, over a lifetime, over a week or even during the 24 hours that constitute a day and thus becomes invisible and not counted in the national income calculations of underdeveloped countries.

The most important point here is that, while women's contribution to the national income is not fully recognized by the international and national development agencies for the fear of providing benefits to them, the attention is diverted by advocating the involvement of women in a big way in the development programmes, mostly as own account workers and voluntary workers.

Role of the United Nations in Involving Women in the Development Programmes

United Nations as an organization has not been particularly successful in influencing the direction and pattern of development of the member nations. However, its major contribution has been to the promotion of some liberal thinking on development issues and gender equity issues in development. The issue of women in development started with the pathbreaking book of Easter Boserup's *Women's Role in Economic Development*, published in 1970.[4]

United Nations took an active interest in integrating women into development. Declaration on the elimination of discrimination against women, World Conference on Women, Programme of Concerted International Action for Advancement of Women are some of the early contributions of the United Nations that sought to promote women's interests development processes. Later UN took active interest in adding women to the development programmes in all the old and newly created branches of UN such as FAO, UNFPA, UNDP, UNICEF, UNESCO, ESCAP, ILO and so on. Thus, the credit for advocating involvement of women in development programmes goes to UN. UN contribution is twofold. On the one hand, it promoted research on women in the context of development and secondly, it facilitated the idea of involving women in development programmes. The essential original objective of Women in Development (WID) was to plan for gender equity in development plans. The target segments were education, training, employment, health, maternity protection and visibility in public life.[5]

Belief of the nations and societies that development is essentially gender neutral has been blamed for the failure of the approach and then the attention of the UN shifted to Gender and Development (GAD) as against women only programmes and finally it shifted to Gender Mainstreaming (GM). The process has started in seventies as gender and development and continued through the eighties and nineties as gender and development and now at the turn of the century as gender mainstreaming. The major difference is that as against the women only approach of WID, the GAD approach aims at planning separately for women and men, taking into consideration the needs, priorities, conceived gender roles, differential capacities of the men and women into consideration. Gender mainstreaming aims at incorporating gender dimensions in all the policies, plans and programmes related to the development process. The United Nations thus played a major role in pushing the idea of women's involvement in development and made it acceptable to all the governments and other aid organizations, such as World Bank, Asian Development Bank, Department for International Development, Government of UK, and host of other aid agencies.[6] We shall refer to all of them including the government and non-governmental organizations involved in development programmes as development advocates.

The development advocates have looked into all the aspects of a woman's life and brought out modules of programme that promoted what is ideal for a women's sustenance in the natural environment such as involvement in community work, care of natural resources, participation in political bodies, economic participation in micro enterprises, provisioning of credit, and so on. Non-governmental organizations have been involved into work as mediators between the development advocates and the poor women. It is because the development advocates cannot reach the target group of poorest women, as the administrative cost of reaching the poorest is rather high. A number of non-governmental organizations worked closely with village communities particularly with generous funding provided by the international aid agencies.

Role of the Government in Involving Women in the Rural Development Programmes

The governments of the Third World countries have imbibed this idea to enlist as many rural women as possible from the poverty groups. Most of the programmes have been successful in including women belonging to the poverty groups, lower castes and tribal communities. Millions of women in the Third World countries have been drawn into this participatory development scenario.

Government of India has gone out of the way to involve rural women in most of the rural development programmes. Women component of the plan and other special schemes for women have been emphasized by the government in the past couple of decades. Attention was paid to allocate 33.5 per cent of the general budgetary allocation across many ministries to the expenditure on the women component in the tenth plan.

Programmes tailor-made for women through self-help groups have been chalked out. Programmes such as Swayamsidha, Swashakti, Swavalamban, Support to Training-cum-Employment Programmes (STEP) and so on aim at providing self-employment to the poor women. Rashtriya Mahila Kosh, the national credit fund for women provides micro credit to women to facilitate self-employment/group enterprise activities. Micro credit programmes are effectively linked to banking institutions, to facilitate two-way flow of funds from the self-help groups to the banks as deposits and from the banks to the self-help groups as loans. Income generation activities are also supported with skill training, technology, market linkups etc. Women are also involved in voluntary work that could bring direct or indirect long-term benefits, such as watershed managements, joint forest management. Government now wants to expand it to the rural health and nutrition programmes. Most of the development programmes integrated micro credit and self-employment initiatives along with watershed development and joint forest management projects.

Encouraged by the isolated successes of the NGO efforts, Community Natural Resource Management has been promoted by the Government of India through 73rd Constitutional Amendment that gives powers to the local self-government (known as Panchayati Raj Institutions or PRIs). They are often referred to as examples of grass-roots level democracy. The local governments could implement schemes of natural resource conservation and management such as social forestry, farm forestry and watershed development.

The government schemes provided part of the funding required, subject to cash and kind contributions from the local governments. It has elaborate guidelines for 33 per cent representation of women in PRIs and on all the committees and councils formed for natural resource management particularly in joint forest management and watershed development. There is also a provision to appoint one or more NGOs to promote community activities, form self-help groups and to enlist women from poor and disadvantaged social groups.

Very few PRIs have taken the initiative. The women representation was good only in the state of Kerala, where the women's literacy rate is very high. In many village communities, there was no incentive to undertake any natural resource conservation on their own. However, what has happened was that a number of women self-help groups have been registered, since the targets to the government officials were set in terms of the number of groups registered. While funding is provided for the capital component of the work, the actual labour input is expected to be put in by the community. This often comes from the women belonging to the poverty groups and lower social rungs.

Roles Assigned to Women in Participatory Development Programmes and Implications to Gender Equity

The NGOs provided variety of opportunities to the women's groups to participate in the natural resource management. Critical tasks were assigned to the women's groups. Conflict resolution with vested interests, negotiations with government authorities, legal battles for control of community lands have all been taken up by the committed NGOs in some instances. The conflict resolution is not always favourable to the poverty groups.

In some of the cases claimed to be successful, often land or resources identified in specific areas were assigned to the women's groups to take up conservation works such as farming, farm forestry, social forestry, tree planting, raising nurseries, collection of non-timber forest produce, etc., in joint forest management programmes. In watershed management programmes, earth work such as desilting of tanks, levelling, bunding, construction of check dams etc., has been taken up by the community and mostly women contributed to manual labour on voluntary basis. When the irrigation management is taken up by the community in activities such as collective provisioning of water, or clearing and widening the canals and field channels, women belonging to the poorer sections are burdened with voluntary manual labour. Sometimes unpaid supervisory work, and monitoring work falls on the women belonging to the middle classes, on behalf of their husbands' interests, while men finally enjoy the benefits of irrigation via increased crop production.[7]

Even in the instances where women are given some plots of land that benefit from irrigation, the women do not normally get the ownership rights of land but only user rights. Women are sometimes given training in sustainable farming practises and production of organic fertilizers such as vermi-compost and so on. Women were given training in skills related to the use of new technology of farming to enhance land productivity, conserving water, generating tree cover and fuel wood bushes and so on. Sometimes they are also trained in growing saplings of specific tree species, for the forest department.[8] Side by side literacy was spread, and women were given sufficient skills to manage the affairs, made aware of their legal rights.

Some of the programmes have shown success in the natural resource conservation. Women were mobilized in large numbers and the conserved resources were allowed to be managed by the women's groups, sometimes among themselves and sometimes among the entire village. There was also considerable personal benefit to the women in terms of farm produce, water, fuel and fodder they could use. Other activities that helped subsistence agriculture such as seed banks, grain banks and micro credit were promoted. The entire package of activities earmarked in the project was closely monitored.[9]

The Success and Failure of Women's Participatory Approach in Natural Resource Management

Let us first differentiate between the community conservation of natural resources which occurs due to communities' own initiative such as 'Chipko' movement in Uttar Pradesh,[10] and the initiatives taken by the governments, aid agencies and the NGOs in bringing the women together and forming self-help groups and training them and assigning them physical work as well as administrative and supervisory work. There are many examples of villagers' own initiatives which normally result in successful community conservation of the natural resources.[11] NGOs may have been involved in such efforts but the initial initiative comes from the community and not the NGOs or the government or the aid agency.

The achievements of such development activities in natural resource management promoted by development advocates are often elaborated in terms of area conserved, contribution made by women for the overall benefits that accrued to the village. Participation itself is considered as a biggest achievement, considering that most of these women are illiterate and belong to the lower social cadres and poverty groups. The gain in knowledge regarding the work they handled, the nuances of dealing with village bodies and local and state government machinery is often the biggest achievement cited. Further, the acceptance of the men in the village of the women's work that brought benefit to the families both directly and indirectly has been listed as an achievement.

Most of the projects worked very well during the stages of monitoring by the NGOs. Once the international agencies stop the funding and the NGOs withdraw and shift to a new location, the activities collapse, due to lack of funds and monitoring. Secondly, women put in their hard labour on lands for which they have no legal rights of either ownership or occupation. Third, the divisive forces in the community such as caste, class and gender often act as deterrents in the long run.

Limited success is possible only in tribal communities that are more cohesive and culturally more equitable gender roles exist by tradition. Fourth, the changing economic scenario, where old skills are redundant, the younger generation is moving away from traditional knowledge and lifestyles even in the villages, making subsistence livelihoods of the type promoted much more difficult. Last but not the least important factor is that the seeming success of sustaining the subsistence livelihoods was not due to the intensive struggle of the women in the groups, formed through a learning process but due to the influence of the NGOs and sometimes due to the influence of the aid agencies behind them. The assumption that five or ten years of support would make the efforts self-sustaining does not hold good, due to the very subsisting nature of the activities and lack of economies of scale.

The Unpaid Work of Women in the Name of Participation in NRM Projects

The contribution of women is always manual hard labour for days, months and sometimes probably years. Most of the studies, even those that claim success acknowledge the fact that the participation in development has increased the burden of work on women involved in it. Both the non-governmental projects and governmental projects had gone on record about the growing burden of women engaged in community activities.[12]

There are no estimates of the value of labour put in by these women and the value of foregone opportunities of wage labour during the period of engagement on voluntary natural resource conservation work. There is no assessment of the hours of household work foregone for the community work and hours of extra work they need to put in to fulfil their household duties such as the care of children, care of the elderly and other household chores such as cooking, cleaning, care of livestock, work on their own farms and so on. The labour protection standards and safety measures and social security do not apply to the voluntary work.

There was no assessment of the value of the actual benefit that accrued to them both monetary as well non-monetary benefits that could be valued. Time saved in fetching water, fuel wood etc., due to natural resource conservation is not assessed. There was no assessment of the value of skills gained by them or their relevance for sustaining livelihoods in future. There is no assessment of the bargaining capacities earned by them to survive in a hostile environment. The process of forming women's groups became more important than the achievement of the goals of upward mobility, enhanced incomes and sustainable livelihoods. Leaving alone the benefits to the women involved, the extent of natural resource conservation achieved is negligible.

While natural resource conservation is promoted on the one hand, the commercial activities that exploited the natural resources in an unsustainable manner were not controlled. For example in Orissa, where NGOs are working for sustainable livelihoods of tribal people, commercial felling of the trees continues, despite the legislations to the contrary. Commercial leases of land for mining of bauxite exist in the dense forest areas of Madhya Pradesh. In rain-fed semi-arid areas of Andhra Pradesh, while watershed management is promoted on the one hand, groundwater has been leased in bottling industry. Overexploitation of the natural resources for the commercial benefits of vested interest continue at large scale, while the conservation efforts are successful in a small way in limited pockets. Thus in the long run, community participation in NRM losses its relevance if the net impact is that of large-scale overexploitation.

Micro Credit

From the early seventies, the women's movements recognized credit as one of the major constraints to women's ability to earn income through self-employment. Banks are unwilling to extend credit to women without regular earnings and without collateral. Collective saving and thrift societies have been able to offer the credibility of joint group collateral of savings and get credit. This practise has helped to discover an entire new era of micro finance, once it is found that the default levels of women's credit groups are very low.

It may look incredible as to what made micro credit a success when the cooperative thrift and credit societies giving loans at the lowest possible interest rates in rural India have failed miserably! Is it the women that made the difference? What is the moral obligation of women to repay, when men who take cooperative loans defaulted? The answer is simple. There is sort of moral pressure applied from within the groups to repay. Moreover, since it is a group effort, default of one person makes the group suffer by closing down future avenues of credit. Similarly, there is also a pressure on keeping the deposit levels reasonably high to maintain the joint collateral. For example, in some credit groups promoted by NGOs it is said that women in the group are expected to contribute one rupee a day or Rs 7 a week towards deposits irrespective of the fact whether they are getting any earning or not!

The high level of repayment caught the attention of all. It is enthusiastically welcomed by United Nations, international aid agencies and the Government of India. Now the private banking sector wants to take advantage of it. Everybody jumped on the bandwagon of micro credit and NGO's have been especially encouraged to form self-help groups and micro finance institutions.

It is welcomed by United Nations and other donor agencies because it dovetailed beautifully with the United Nations' new understanding of the importance of informal economy, which involved poor and marginalized people. Donor agencies were happy because repayments reduced their burden of financing for poverty reduction. It also offered an entry point to the informal sector Bottom of the Pyramid (BoP) consumer. It enthused the government since it found yet another avenue of rural credit after having failed all the other avenues of credit such as cooperatives, nationalized banks and commercial banks. All the financial institutions which are flooded with funds found avenues of profitable lending. Hence, large number of NGOs have been roped into the formation of micro credit organizations. NGOs in turn used women who worked voluntarily in the movement to bring other women. Smooth working of the micro finance institutions is ensured by the government, with well-established links to

NABARD, establishment of Rashtriya Mahila Kosh or National Credit Fund for Women. Commercial banks encouraged by the donor agencies intend to come into the sector of micro finance in a big way. NGOs financed by donor agencies and the government's own machinery promoted micro finance.

Micro credit is projected as the economic super highway for women's upward mobility and rural poverty reduction. As a result, the more important interventions that are designed to create jobs, social welfare grants and social security for women have taken a back seat on the UN agenda as well as the government agenda. For the UN and the other donor agencies such as USAID, World Bank, micro finance and self-help group formation has become an entry point. It is easy to add the other development agendas of health and poverty reduction. It fitted into the new economic paradigm of financial self-sustainability. The model of micro finance also fits into the privatization and linking of the poor to capital markets and removal of subsidies of all sorts, making people pay.

Advantages and Disadvantages of Micro Credit

One single most important achievement of the micro credit is to make credit available at an interest rate lower than that of the local moneylender without any collateral. However, this did not seem to prevent the women from falling into the debt trap of money lending. Since it is informal credit, in times of need, families borrow from every single source they can. Since micro credit is not available in large amounts for consumption purpose, families also borrow from moneylenders. Beyond any doubt, the micro credit could not protect the rural families from falling into the clutches of the moneylenders. It is one more avenue of credit and often bankrupt women borrowed from moneylenders to repay the self-help group.

Soon the problems of micro credit came to the fore. The view that micro finance leads to individual economic empowerment, social and economic well-being is challenged. Research and evaluation studies revealed that such assumptions are wrong. The micro enterprises have always not been successful. The rural environment for the success of micro enterprises depends upon the economic fundamentals. Such investment opportunities and skills are prevalent in rural areas. As per the mid-term appraisal of the Tenth Plan, (RMK) The Rashtryia Mahila Kosh has been able maintain a recovery of 90 per cent of the loans. However, out of an outlay of 143 crore, only 43.63 crore were sanctioned for micro finance and out of this only 29.55 crore were disbursed. This shows the inability of micro finance to be a vehicle of investment in rural areas. Organizations such as SEWA have their own bank, their own insurance company and their own paid staff to promote the micro enterprises among women. Despite this integration, and constant flow of money for development activities, the organization's reach is limited.

Women often used the borrowing for the family business run by the men. They also take consumption loans for family uses such as health care and other household assets. It is often found that while the repayment burden is on the women, men enjoyed the benefits of credit. Ironically, micro credit created instances of women shackled in debt rather than independent successful women entrepreneurs.

Implications to Gender Equity and Socio-economic Advancement: Areas of Further Research

The poor and disadvantaged women in the rural areas are the targets. They are normally illiterate, less informed and easily drawn into the development work without questioning. The only visible impact in some parts of India was the formation of a large number of self-help groups. Probably some amount of space has been created for women to spend time outside the homes without male domination. This is not to say that women's participation should not be promoted, but to say that unless the participatory approach undergoes a drastic change from mere formation of groups to that of making them demand their fair share of development, the benefits of participation would be undermined. It is not clear how it can translate into negotiating power in future.

An important achievement claimed has been the act of drawing women out of their homes and providing them an opportunity to work on the issues of community interest, which is expected to broaden their outlook and decision-making capacity. Mostly natural resource management programmes are found be more successful when tribal women are involved. Tribal communities particularly give more freedom to the women than other village communities. Some of the social gains of participation by way of freedom and control and household decision-making in this context are probably more imaginary than real.

Ultimately, one has to judge the benefits of participation from the net economic benefit that accrued to the women equality of opportunity achieved and finally the strength of bargaining power gained through group formation. If there are no substantial benefits on all these fronts, the participatory approach to development need to be revisited.

However, much more research is needed on this subject of participatory development in the context of women; given the fact that a space is created for women outside the homes and said to be appreciated and valued by the women in the group, despite negligible impact on natural resource conservation and poverty alleviation. The future effort is to examine how this could be transformed into a negotiating strength for better livelihoods for women.

One would like to ask and get an answer as to how much of this response to the call to come out of their homes and participate in community work is facilitated by increasing female literacy and aspirations of economic gain? Another important point often not acknowledged is that the work participation of women in poverty groups is always high and the wage earned, though very meagre is in their control. There is no achievement in drawing women into work, since traditionally poor women's work participation rates at exploitative wage rates are very high. Hence, they are easily drawn into the community work for meagre gains.

One would like to know, how much of this so-called skill empowerment in management, micro credit administration, crop production, and other self-employment activities, translates into long lasting employment opportunities to bring about upward economic mobility? Even if the training is successful, even if women have acquired the skills, if there is no market for their administrative, managerial and other skills they possess, the women will not benefit. Thus, the skills imparted may be useful to the project but may not be useful for sustaining their livelihoods. The viability of the micro credit and micro enterprises in the fast changing world needs further probe.

Increase in female literacy and work participation gave some level of freedom of decision-making in a limited manner to women in all communities and especially to the rural women in the southern parts of India. This should not be confused with empowerment due to participation in development programmes.

Notes

1. Foreword written by A.K. Sen to the book by Devaki Jain, *Women, Development and the UN*.
2. Jean Dreze and Amartya Sen, *India: Development and Participation*.
3. Time use Surveys.
4. Devaki Jain, *Women, Development and the UN, United Nations Intellectual History Project Series,* Indian University Press, 2005.
5. Devaki Jain, op. cit.
6. FAO, regional office for Asia and the Pacific, "Learning Resource Gender and Women in Agriculture and Rural Development in Asia", 2004.
7. Priti Rammurthy, "Rural Women and Irrigation, Patriarchy, Class and the Modernizing State I South India", in *Women Working in the Environment,* edited by Carolyn. E. Sachs.
8. Women self-help groups in Karikal in Tamil Nadu are involved in the production of mangrove saplings sold to the forest departments. It is a seasonal activity.
9. Neera Bura, UNDP India, "Empowering Women for Household Food security", 2004 (Mimeo) also see, Aga Khan Foundation, "Understanding women's Experience in Natural Resource Management" (Private circulation) 1999.
10. R. Ahas, T. Puura, A. Janssen and E. Peter (eds.), 1999, Boreal Forests of the World IV: Integrating Cultural Values into Local and Global

Forest Protection. Proceedings of the 4th Biannual Conference of the Taiga Rescue Network, October 5-10, 1998, Tartu, Estonia, Estonian Green Movement, Tartu, Parts 1 and 2.

11. See Appendix.
12. Evaluation Report of the Andhra Pradesh Rural Livelihood Programme (Mimeograph).

Appendix
Self-Initiated Movements of Community Conservation

Most of the successful cases of natural resource management were by local organizations rooted in tradition or through modified traditional systems or new organizations developed in response to a particular situation.

Some of the most successful natural resource conservation movements were self-initiated. When the interests of the community and the outside society are openly diverse, community-based natural resource conservation measures are born out of the struggle of the communities fighting against commercial exploitation of natural resources. Such recent examples are protection of forest area against commercial exploitation by Gonda tribal community struggle in Maharashtra, *in situ* conservation of hundreds of varieties of traditional food crops in Uttaranchal, struggle of the tribal communities to save 700 ha. of grassland from limestone mining, protecting the habitat of sea turtle in Kerala, and protection of the nestling sites of spot bill pelican in Karnataka, sacred groves in temple areas of Tamil Nadu, and so on. Natural resource protection in such cases is site specific. The local norms and regulations are responsible for the collective action. Women are actively involved in these movements.

8 Local Governance Institutions and Citizen Leadership

A Means to Promote Participatory Development: A PRIA Experience in Mahabubnagar District of AP

Praveen Sriramshetty

The 73rd Constitutional Amendment has given space and opportunity to the poor and marginalized to participate and own the decision-making processes of development at the grass roots through three-tier Panchayati Raj system. The enactment to have local governing institutions elected through mandatory processes has definitely brought a significant social change and impact on grass-roots development. This has promoted different sections of the society to participate and involve in decision-making processes. This has bought new evolutions and meaning to the terms development and participation. The term 'development' is understood differently over the years from service delivery to means of empowerment in the changing national and global contexts of socio-political, cultural and economic environment. Today, development is not looked at in isolation addressing sectoral issues but it includes a complex range of issues that are interwoven. Today, we can see citizens raising their collective voice to access resources in view of the economic liberalization and realize the economic benefits are being enjoyed by few while leaving the majority in exclusion. So did the meaning of participation shifted to ownership of development through meaningful engagement to demand accountability. Moreover, there is also a paradigm shift in the role of the state as from provider to facilitator in post-globalization scenario.

In this context, it becomes imperative to see development in relation to citizen participation. It brings into focus the relationship between the state and its deprived citizens and raises a critical question of how deprived citizens can be actors. This needs conditions for playing active role by the deprived sections in the local governance institutions, which is still not in their reach. The role of civil society comes into fore for facilitating the processes for creating conducive environment for the marginalized to participate in the development at the grass roots. In these circumstances it becomes imperative to the civil society to facilitate the process for devolution of powers to the local bodies, while strengthening the capacities of the citizens and elected representatives to take over the development process through local governance. In 1950s, the government concept was welfare-oriented and in 1970s it was changed to development-oriented. In the 1990s and the post globalization, the development concept emerged as empowerment-oriented. Then local governance institutions and empowerment aspects were tried to address through 73rd and 74th Constitutional Amendment Act, which provide scope to intervene non-governmental organizations.

Enactment of law and the proactive role of civil society in last one and a half decade have created opportunity for citizen participation and there was realization for raising collective efforts hence led to the emergence of collective efforts to amplify the voices of the citizens particularly the marginalized and socially disabled (women, dalits and adivasis). Citizen collectives have been seen as a means for pressure building, mobilizing and influencing the state and seeking their presence in the decision-making processes. In the present context, the promotion of collective groups among various social groups resulted in development of new citizen leadership.

Citizen Leaders, Citizen Collectives and Local Governance Institutions

Citizen leader is resident of the local community with a vision and commitment towards the development of the community who can motivate and is able to mobilize community on issues affecting the lives of people. Who has the qualities to identify and analyze the issues and can also provide innovative solutions to the issues. He can act as a bridge between the community and the external actors. Citizen leader can make a visible difference in the community with his/her presence and understanding on the issues. At the same time, he is a useful resource for the external agencies to access the community.

Role of Citizen Leader

A citizen leader needs to perform many roles but primarily the following two roles are important.

Community Building

1. *Mobilization*: Primarily, a citizen leader should mobilize the poor and marginalized sections towards their involvement in the decision-making processes of governance. The purpose of mobilization may vary from engaging in constructive development work to large-scale protest activities. A citizen leader needs to include vulnerable/deprived/disadvantaged sections of the society in the mainstream who were invisible and voiceless till now.
2. *Negotiate*: The citizen leader needs to deal with the varied views and thoughts. They need to manage these and resolve the conflicts emerging within the community. This could be through negotiations and decisions acceptable to all.

Engaging Governance Institutions

Another major role of the citizen leader is to engage with different institutions towards reforming governance for the development of society/community.

1. A citizen leader helps in raising *voices* on emerging issues affecting the community at large through different forums and forms like Gram Sabha and citizen collectives.
2. Citizen leader represents the community in voicing the concerns and plays a role of a *negotiator* for an amicable solution between the community and local institutions with social consciousness.
3. A citizen leader must build his *credibility* among the community. This factor is earned. If promised to be present on some occasions, it is to be fulfilled whatever difficulties may come. It highlights the principle 'what he/she says, does also'.

Participatory Development

PRIA's believes in engaging civil society in the form of citizen leadership and various forms of networks, committees towards reforming governance institutions, by the use of participatory mechanisms. These are being implemented through its field level

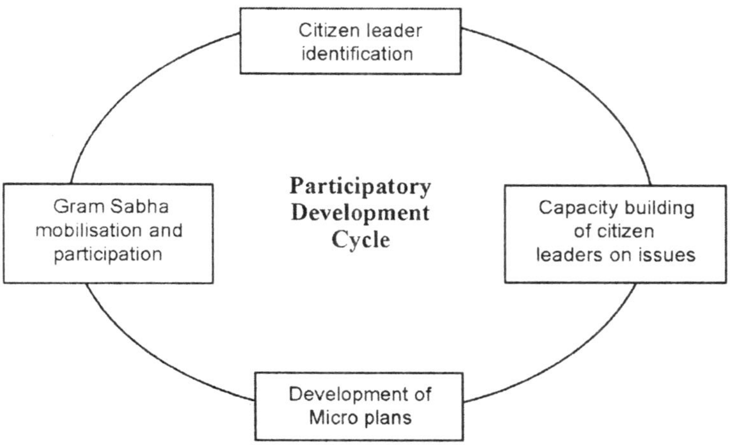

interventions with the community, elected representatives (ERs), citizen collectives (CCs) and PRI functionaries.

The above cycle is being adopted in one of the interventional districts i.e. Mahabubnagar in Andhra Pradesh. The cycle has been divided into four stages: (1) Citizen leader identification, (2) Capacity building of citizen leaders on issues, (3) Development of micro plans, (4) Gram sabha mobilization and participation.

Citizen Leader Identification

Identification of citizen leader is an important aspect as he/she plays a vital role in promoting the participation of the community in the development processes. The leaders are identified on the basis of their participation in the meetings, understanding about issues, ability to convince people, and leadership qualities etc. In the primary stage, Community-Based Organizations (CBOs) are being formed by mobilizing the community. These groups meet on regular intervals to discuss issues affecting their lives and derive appropriate strategies to address them.

Capacity Building

It is believed that all persons are born with certain natural in-built qualities. There are certain qualities which one needs to posses to exude leadership. These qualities need to be nurtured so as to convert them into skills like communication, decision-making, strategizing, analyzing, ability to innovate, influencing, etc., for use into practical situations. This process leads to the emergence of a citizen leader.

Capacity building of citizen leaders on forms of mobilization has been taken up in our intensive panchayats in Khillaghanpur mandal of Mahabubnagar to strengthen the capacities of identified citizen leaders to effectively participate in all the governance issues of gram panchayat and play an important role in addressing the issues.

Series of orientation programmes were organized for citizen leaders (CL) and citizen collectives (CC) in the district. The initial phase of orientation programme was focusing on:

- Motivate the citizen leaders on the importance of gram sabha and their role in mandatory gram sabha.
- Raising the issues of common citizens and influencing the elected representatives of gram panchayat to work towards addressing the same.
- To enhance the participation of the women and dalits and put forward their issues in mandatory gram sabhas through collective action.
- To encourage citizen leaders to become elected representatives for PRIs to get quality leadership.

Personality Development

The workshops focused on issues like qualities of a good leader, body language, interpersonal relationship, trust, confidence building, addressing the public, leadership styles etc. Modules were developed pertaining to these aspects and used in the workshops in the form of role plays, games, exercises etc.

Gender Mainstreaming

Gender mainstreaming was considered an important aspect to prevent discrimination of any kind among them from different socio-cultural backgrounds. The focused areas covered are gender roles, power equations, gender empowerment etc.

Development of Micro Plans

The plan for the smallest unit of administration i.e., panchayat is called a micro plan. In this method, the gram sabha members of each ward plan for their own ward. These ward level plans may be named as people's plan. These people's plans are put together to make a panchayat level plan and are called micro plans. The problems faced by villagers are solved through solutions that they feel comfortable with. Each problem is solved at the local level with the participation of the gram sabha members, elected representatives, government officials and others.

- It involves participation of citizens/ERs and government representatives.
- It builds linkages with other tier PRIs to enhance institutional relations as well as get funds for micro plan implementation.
- It promotes roles to be played by citizens, ERs, and concerned authorities.
- Promotes ownership.
- People's participation brings in accountability and transparency.
- Enhances judicious use of resources.
- Common understanding on issues of the village identified.
- Integrated long-term planning at lowest level is developed
- Participation in development processes.
- Participatory decision-making.

The Micro Plan will involve that you:

- Organize the gram sabha members and the panchayats to go through the stages of mapping resources in the geographical spread of the panchayat.
- Analyze the cause and effect of the problems and motivate all to think of solutions.
- Prepare the plan and the budget together.
- Get it sanctioned in gram sabha.
- Submit it to different departments.

Gram Sabha Mobilization and Participation

Gram sabhas are the nuclei to the decentralized decision-making process where it is known as general body meeting in which progress of the previous gram sabha decisions is reviewed and plan for the future course of action. In this scenario, it becomes all the more important to make the community realize the importance to take part in these processes. However, the community does not realize the need to get involved in the mandatory gram sabhas primarily due to ignorance, access and dynamics of the community. Here the role of the citizen leader and citizen collective's becomes important in mobilizing for the participation in the gram sabha. At times different sections of the community may oppose the move. Hence, sensitization of the community on issues and participation in development becomes imperative.

The main objective of these programmes is to build common perspectives on issues and its impact on the society particularly the marginalized. Special focus was given on gram sabha, its functioning and its role in the decision-making process was shared with CLs, mock gram sabha exercises were organized to make them familiar with functions of gram sabhas. They were encouraged to participate in micro plans and follow it up in the mandatory gram sabhas. Meetings are held to orient regarding any new scheme, act enforced by the state and how they can avail of the benefits.

Following are some exemplars of citizen leaders promoting participatory development process.

Exemplars

Mr. Hanumanthu, who is the Deputy Sarpanch of Md. Hussainpally of Khillghanpur Mandal. He is very active participant of PRIA orientation programmes and he is also the member of ward members' network. During the gram sabha mobilization in the month April 2004, sarpanch was reluctant to conduct the gram sabha. Mr. Hanumanthu with the help of villagers and other ward members pressurized the sarpanch to organize the gram sabha. This is the first incidence where gram sabha was organized in the panchayat. Till date regular gram sabhas are conducted in the panchayat and they are successfully able to resolve the issues like drinking water for the panchayat.

Mrs. Kondamma exudes leadership among the women in the SHG and the GP. She attended all the meetings organized by PRIA and says she has found another way to move her group forward i.e., use the women's 'group pressure' to handle social issues. In order to address livelihood issues of women in the village, she gave a call to the women to coordinate and pressurize the sarpanch and mandal officials to start a milk centre at the village. This ensures that SHG women can sell the cattle's milk, earn a livelihood and contribute to savings. In order to prevent any corruption at the milk booth, they appointed an educated woman to maintain the accounts and showed her a source of livelihood within the village.

Mrs. Meera Bai from Mahabubnagar was actively involved in rendering services to the community and helped many families in availing benefits under different schemes of the government at the village level. She disseminates information about new schemes towards helping the needy and the poor at the ward level to improve their conditions. She is dynamic and outspoken in various matters relating to the municipality level functioning. The women groups and the community in general saw in Meera Bai a leader who understood their needs and could do much to improve their conditions.

Conclusion

In the post-decentralization scenario and changing face of socio-economic and political situation, participation in the development processes has taken a new shape towards a social change. Emergence of new leadership especially from the poor and marginalized to mention 33 per cent reservation to women in PRIs has provided space and opportunity to access and control over resources. The approach followed in Mahabubnagar district for participating in the decision-making at the lowest levels. The main challenge faced was from the community itself since the community is the formation of individuals belonging to different socio-economic political strata. Having a common understanding on issues in itself poses a big challenge as the impact of the issue on citizens varies.

9 Dimensions of NGOs Working with Women and Children in Rajasthan

Jyotsana Rajvanshi

The present paper is based on the assessment report of the project conducted on Networking of Organizations with Women and Children in Rajasthan in coordination with UNICEF Rajasthan. The project included two sections i.e., first was the assessment and observation report of NGOs and the other was compilation of information of NGOs in the form of a resource directory. NGOs in Rajasthan are doing various activities for the last few decades to improve status of women and children, a compilation of their details in appropriate format and shift in their activities was needed for a ready reference to facilitate networking role of NGOs. With the objective of networking, NGOs willing to translate women and child rights into action, an assessment report of NGOs giving background of development of NGO in Rajasthan has been prepared. Looking at the dimensions of NGOs their role can be clearly identified.

Jyotsana Rajvanshi, NGOs: Structure, Operation and Vision, Research Report No. 95, IDSJ, 1999.

Background

NGOs are an important part of civil society and they work at grass-roots level directly among people. They play an important role in implementation of programmes by associating people directly at the village level. NGOs were associated in developmental programmes after Seventh Plan, which contained a separate chapter on NGOs. The Eighth Plan document clearly specified that "voluntary organizations can act as a catalyst and can organize beneficiaries, involve people in planning and development and provide necessary support to make development a reality". The Ninth Plan even earmarked priority areas of primary education, health for all, drinking water, housing and rural road construction for channelizing people's participation for meaningful rural development. Thus, the policy of the government has been to work in close partnership with the NGOs for the achievement of social and economic goals enshrined in our constitution.

The government has also encouraged the involvement of international voluntary agencies through coordinating organizations like the Central Social Welfare Board (CSWB) and the People's Action for Development (PAD), presently known as the Council for Advancement for People's Action for Rural Technology (CAPART). In pre-independence era, almost all the NGOs were not getting assistance from the state or foreign donors. It has been envisaged that growth of NGOs is not uniform over the years; for example, after 1947 the number of NGOs increased slowly but after the decision of Planning Commission regarding the involvement of NGOs with government organisations and introducing provision of certain amendments i.e., Section 35 CC (1977) and Section 35 CCA in the Indian Income Tax Act. The number of NGOs increased rapidly but the geographical distribution is not uniform, most importantly it may be due to availability of infrastructure facilities and other resources in developed regions.

The rise in number of NGOs has also been the contribution made by international/national efforts. India ratified CEDAW in 1993 and CRC in 1992 and committed to secure equal rights of women and equal rights of children in India. Main objective of the directory is networking of NGOs and government organizations willing to translate women and child rights into action because the status of women and children is very low in Rajasthan. Their subordination is culturally constructed and maintained at material and ideological levels—each reinforcing the other. The historical legacy of feudalism and patriarchal structures has also influenced women's life in the society. Since 1980s the Government of Rajasthan has initiated a number of programmes for development and empowerment of women and children. The convention on the Rights of the Child emphasizes social reintegration of child victims, to the extent possible, without resorting to judicial proceedings. Hence, to ensure optimum growth and development of children we need to cater to needs of these especially underprivileged children.

The Central Social Welfare Board (CSWB in 1953), State Level Social Welfare Advisory Boards and a Backward Classes Welfare Department (1951–1952) was established to promote welfare and development services for women and children especially from the marginalized and underprivileged groups. The department was renamed as the Social Welfare Department in 1956 by the inclusion of social welfare activities. The department coordinated several activities for women's and child welfare i.e., homes, training and rehabilitation of women in distress, hostels for working women, shelters and training schemes. In 1975, the Integrated Child Development Services (ICDS) were also entrusted to it.

During the post-independence period most of the programmes largely focussed on women welfare. The Report of the Committee on Status of Women in India pointed out for adverse sex ratio, rural female infant mortality rate, low mean age at marriage, and having the lowest literacy rate both in urban and rural areas in Rajasthan. The Sixth Five-Year Plan (1980–85) focused on health, education and employment of women. Subsequently, during the Seventh Plan period in 1985 a separate Department of Women and Children and Nutrition was established. Various programmes being run by other departments were then brought under this department. State Policy for Women (2000) and National Policy for Children was announced and a number of women's development programmes have implemented in Rajasthan in the spheres of health, education and rural employment in Rajasthan. The Women's Development Programme for Economic Development of Women included direct intervention for poverty eradication, Self-Help Groups (SHGs), Sampooran Gram Rozgar Yojna, Swaran Jayanti Swarozgar Yojna, Mahila Smridhi Yojna, Indira Mahila Swayam Sidha Yojna, Rashtriya Mahila Kosh, Free Training and Employment Schemes (STEP/NORAD). DPEP under Sarva Shiksha Abhiyan is linking girls in education through Kasturba Girls Schools and mobile schools.

Before the establishment of DWCD, NGOs were definitely working for education and health activities of women and children. It was in 1980s that NGOs came up for support and advocacy of issues like women and child development. After establishment of separate department of women and children, some NGOs took up ICDS blocks for providing nutrition to children by running Anganwadi centres. NGOs included in the directory are now closely associated with education, health of women and children, immunization, nutrition activities, rural sanitation, formation of self-help groups and training for self-employment according to the information given by them in the format. But there is still a wider scope of skill development for self-employment and income generation activities, legal awareness about rights of women and children, rehabilitation of handicapped women and children, removal of social evils, starting night schools for child labour, running of Bal Ashram for orphan children on the pattern of widow homes where NGOs' active services are required for the welfare of women and children, as informed by the NGOs. There has been increasing recognition by the international human rights movement of the gap between the principle of universality and the actualizing of women's human rights. In view of protecting women against violence and recent Supreme Court judgment, human rights of women have gained more importance. Few NGOs came forward to protect women against gender discrimination and advocate as well as protect their legal rights by creating awareness among them. A few NGOs are working on violence and atrocities against women.

Rationale

NGOs in Rajasthan are doing various activities from the last few decades to improve status of women and children, a compilation of their details in appropriate format and shift in their activities was needed for a ready reference to facilitate networking role of NGOs. With the objective of networking, NGOs willing to translate women and child rights into action, an assessment report of NGOs and Resource Directory of NGOs has been prepared. Institute of Development Studies had compiled in 1996 a directory of NGOs working in 31 districts of Rajasthan. Subsequently, it was updated also in 1999. It contained 452 NGOs working in different areas. Since then many more NGOs have entered the field during last 5 years. From time to time, other directories of NGOs have also been published.

Information is based on the formats sent by NGO concerned. Effort has been made to update correct information in this directory and full care has been taken to ensure its correctness. It describes the work of wide range of organizations including small and large both. It is not claimed that the organizations included in the directory are better than others not included in the directory. None can be inferior to the other.

Most of the NGOs had highlighted the problem of lack of financial resources as a hindrance in implementation of their objectives. Hence, a directory of funding agencies for child and women, programmes as well as information regarding UN agencies related to NGOs have also been added as Annexure I and II respectively. Directory of funding agencies include funding ministries, government funding agencies, non-government funding agencies, embassies and loaning agencies along with schemes of women and children for which assistance can be obtained.

The main *objectives* of the project were as under:

- Networking of NGOs and government organizations willing to translate women and child rights into action.

- To document a comprehensive overview and available information of the services meant for women and children conducted by NGOs in Rajasthan.
- To reveal the gaps in services available for women and children
  - Groups of children agewise/genderwise for which there are no services at present
  - Gaps in intake policies
  - Dialogue with needy community
- To initiate and facilitate a process of dialogue between the needy, community and helplines to share the issues with a view to reach out to the needy women and children in society.
- Current status of NGOs/government organization.
- Prepare district wise directory of NGOs to build local capacity of child and women's organizations to assist the government.

Process of Compiling Resource Directory

It required the systematic compilation of all organizations working with women and children in Rajasthan. It involved the following processes outlined below:

Identifying Existing Sources of Information about Services through

- Existing directories of services
- State Social Welfare Department and Women and Child Development Department.
- Newspapers.
- Word-of-mouth.
- After exploring the sources, a list of organizations was prepared.
- As one proceeded in collecting information, more organizations were added to the list.
- Letters were sent to the identified organizations.

- A format for the collection of data was prepared in consultation with UNICEF.

(i) Format for collection of basic information from NGOs was prepared by the project coordinator for discussion and opinion of experts as well as representatives of departments working in the field of women and child welfare.

(ii) *Round Table Discussion*: A Round Table discussion was organized at IDS on 7th January 2005 to finalize the formats. Experts, academicians, NGO leaders, ex-IAS officers and other concerned persons gave valuable suggestions regarding format to be filled in by respective NGOs for compilation of resource directory.

Process of Collection of Details

A format was prepared to collect information to be completed by respective NGOs on following points:

- Name, address, phone number, e-mail, registration number of NGO.
- Contact person, Chairman and Secretary.
- Area of operation: Urban/Rural including main districts and blocks.
- Number of male and female workers: Paid as well as honorary.
- Main objectives of NGO.
- Ongoing activities/services being undertaken for women and children by NGOs during 2001–2004.
- Future activities/services proposed to be undertaken by NGOs.
- Networking with other NGOs with names.
- Funding agencies along with other sources of finance.
- Suggestions regarding gaps to be covered regarding services for women and children in the state.

Along with registration certificate, memorandum of association, progress reports and certificate from funding departments in the projects.

Sources for Listing Names of NGOs were Identified as under:

- NGO directory prepared by IDSJ in 1996 and 1999 (452 NGOs).
- Letters of NGOs received in IDSJ during 1999–2004 (146 new NGOs).
- List from Directorate of Women and Child, GoR, Jaipur (106 new NGOs).
- List from Directorate of Medical and Health, GoR, Jaipur (5 Mother NGOs).
- List received from CUTS-CART, Jaipur (292 new NGOs).
- List from Rajasthan Hunger Project (25 new NGOs).
- List from Rajasthan Voluntary Health Association (72 new NGOs).
- List from Chairman, NGO Network, Chittorgarh (19 old NGOs).
- Bhoruka Charitable Trust, MNGO for RCH and FP (5 new NGOs).
- Project Director and Deputy Director ICDS, Jhunjhunu (11 new NGOs).
- Environmental NGOs in India (1992) Directory published by Ministry of Environment and Forests, Government of India (187 new NGOs including DAINET directory).
- DAINET (Development Alternatives Information Network) NGO Directory, Volume-IV, Rajasthan (1998), New Delhi.
- Council for Participatory Action for Rural Technology (CAPART) Rajasthan.
- 147 new NGOs.

- District Poverty Initiatives Programme Rajasthan (86 new NGOs).
- *Development Associates* (Resource Manual) (1995), edited by J.P. Malik and Sudhanshu Shekhar Singh, 178/7, Rohini, Sector 2, Delhi-110085.
- A Directory of Funding Agencies for NGOs (2000), by Gopalsingh Kachhwaha, Pratap Nagar, Jodhpur.
- Rajasthan Mein Paryavaran Ke Gair Sarkari Evam Sarkari Prayas Directory (Hindi) (2002), by Pashchim Bharat, Thaltej Tekra, Ahmedabad.
- Directory of Rural Development Institutions in India (2002), NIRD, Rajendra Nagar, Hyderabad. (ed.) K.S. Raju.
- Support Services to Counter Violence Against Women in Rajasthan: A Resource Directory of NGOs (2002) published by IDS in collaboration with UNIFEM South Asia Regional Office.
- Profile 500, Selected Voluntary Organizations in India, (2003) Published by Centre for Advancement of Philanthropy, Mumbai.
- The NGLS Hand Book of UN Agencies, Programmes and Funds working for Economic and Social Development (1994), Published by United Nations Non-Governmental Liaison Services (NGLS).

District Collectors, District Women and Child Department, CMHO, Mother NGOs, District Social Welfare Department, DRDA and other district level departments were contacted and letters were posted to all of them requesting list of NGOs active in the field of women and children in their districts.

Collection of Information

An integrated list was prepared on the basis of information collected from various sources given above.

(a) Letters along with format to be filled by NGOs were sent as per the list given below after tallying with previous lists to avoid duplication of issue of letters. Dispatch of format to NGOs was started immediately thereafter. The letters and contacts were made with NGOs of various districts as under:

	District	*Total NGOs*		*District*	*Total NGOs*
1.	Ajmer	61	17.	Dholpur	18
2.	Alwar	71	18.	Nagaur	27
3.	Udaipur	121	19.	Pali	34
4.	Karauli	25	20.	Barmer	46
5.	Kota	61	21.	Baran	11
6.	Chittorgarh	43	22.	Banswara	14
7.	Churu	34	23.	Bikaner	98
8.	Jaipur	366	24.	Bundi	9
9.	Jalore	11	25.	Bharatpur	72
10.	Jaisalmer	8	26.	Bhilwara	26
11.	Jodhpur	78	27.	Rajsamand	38
12.	Jhalawar	15	28.	Sawai Madhopur	44
13.	Jhunjhunu	49	29.	Sirohi	7
14.	Tonk	42	30.	Sikar	24
15.	Dungarpur	19	31.	Sri Ganganagar	20
16.	Dausa	37	32.	Hanumangarh	16
	Total				1,545

(b) Entry in computer was made as and when complete information was received. Some letters returned back due to change in address or non-availability of NGO. In some cases, incomplete information was received for which fresh reminders were sent by post, e-mail, telephone or personally. Verification certificate from departments was also included to be furnished by NGOs along with other details. (A copy of format and certificate is also enclosed for ready reference.)

Assessment of Activities of NGOs

Field Visit of NGOs working with women and children was conducted by preparing a list by the project coordinator with the help of known NGOs/Sanstha Manch, field level NGO officials in respective districts. The purpose of the visit was to understand the intervention strategy of the organizations, to explain the concept of directory.

Districtwise field visit was arranged by making route chart for assessment and discussion with NGOs. Field workers/research investigators approached the NGOs for field visit in different districts after a discussion with them.

Information Received

Information received from various NGOs was computerized in Hindi as well as English. Almost 500 NGOs responded to the columns given in the format. Resource Directory includes the information given by NGOs themselves.

Assessment and Comprehensive Overview of NGOs Services

Registration

NGOs are considered as 'Social Service Organizations' from the First Five-Year Plan. The analysis of the registration of NGOs shows that, the first NGO established independent of the political process was Vidya Bhavan Society established by Mohan Singh Mehta in Udaipur in the year 1931 with the aim of imparting education. The oldest grass-roots support organization was Seva Mandir, Udaipur and even at present about 20 per cent NGOs of Rajasthan are linked with Seva Mandir as evident from the information received from NGOs of various districts. Prof. John Mathai organized scheduled caste people in Beawar (district Ajmer) for manufacture and export of leather goods in 1960s. The spread of voluntarism in Rajasthan has been the response of urban, middle class, professional people from inside and outside the state. Some of the bureaucrats at the senior level were NGO-friendly; they established a dialogue between Rajasthan government and NGOs. In 1981, it was decided that NGOs would be involved in family planning, social forestry, intensive rural development and education. Thus education, health and family welfare, poverty alleviation and self-employment, environment etc., have been the main objectives of NGOs in Rajasthan since long. Due to government support most of the NGOs were registered during the period 1981–1990 specially in the districts of Jaipur, Jhunjhunu and Barmer also. Highest number of NGOs are registered in Jaipur as evident from the above given districtwise table of NGOs from whom the information was called for. It might have been due to changing government policies for supporting the NGOs. URMUL group of NGOs in Bikaner area also has linkages with many NGOs of the desert area.

During 1991–2000, many more NGOs were registered in Jaipur, Bikaner, Kota, Jodhpur, Ajmer, Alwar, Bharatpur, Tonk. Funds were generally provided to NGOs for government designed schemes of literacy, health, adult education. The other important factor was the easy flow of funds from foreign funding agencies and the provision of exemption from income tax, which was the most facilitative way of working and the registration of greater number of NGOs. Seventh Plan had given special importance to NGOs by including a separate chapter for NGOs. A beginning to associate NGOs in development programmes was made in the Seventh Five-Year Plan.

Objectives and Activities of NGOs

Generally, objectives of the NGOs are based on background of the promoters. The objectives of NGO reflect the scope of activities and the goal of NGO. It can be noticed from the details in the directory that almost all the NGOs have multiple objectives. The maximum number of NGOs almost in every district have their main objectives as education, rural development, self-help group formation, self-employment of women, health of women and children, immunization, nutrition of children, awareness generation of women. A few organizations work for consumer protection, post-literacy programmes, prevention of social evils, drug addiction, home industries, computer training, sanitation, legal awareness, prevention of atrocities against women, education guarantee scheme, Balwadi, Bal Vigyan Mela, creche, work for Viklang, deaf and dumb children also. Few others also work for environment and water conservation. Almost all the districts have more than 70 per cent NGOs with the objectives of welfare including that of education and health of women and children.

Some NGOs work at lowest levels of society, they are community-based. Others are engaged in training, research, information, awareness and IEC activities. There are very few NGOs dealing with creating legal awareness about rights of women or working for widows and running old age day care centre or ashram for them. NGOs running creche for children, thinking of setting schools for child labour are in sufficient number.

A government sponsored NGO, CAPART was created to allot rural development projects only to NGOs for self-employment of women, training of village animators, construction of Indira Avas and sanitary latrines in rural areas and schemes of drinking water supply etc., to develop rural areas with people's participation and through NGOs. Main object was to reduce distance between the government and the people, increase people's participation and implement plans as per needs of people at the grass roots. Forest development committees have been formed amongst the villagers for development of forests in the villages. Wasteland Development Board allotted areas to NGOs for development of forests, pastures and plantation. Soil conservation projects were allotted for soil and water conservation to many NGOs. On the insistence of World Bank, NGOs were also allotted agricultural extension projects to compare government work with NGO efforts. NGOs were actively associated in total literacy mission by associating them with running non-formal literacy centres. Foreign agencies allotted various projects of health and education and empowerment of women to NGOs.

Structure of NGOs

A number of factors have an impact on the performance of NGOs. Specially in case of NGOs working for the welfare of children and women programmes, factors like women members, women office bearers, women workers (paid or honorary) have important bearing on the working efficiency of NGO. It will be observed from the directory that almost in all cases, with only few exceptions, most of the NGOs have almost 50 per cent female members. In some cases, women members are even more than the male members. It indicates a favourable trend. The average number of members is around 10 except in educational NGOs or those having wider area of work.

As regards women office bearers, about 10–15 per cent NGOs only have women as Chairman or Secretary. In exceptional cases only, both the office bearers are females. Almost 80–85 per cent office bearers are males. Even then it seems as a favourable trend. Generally, Secretary or President is the contact person also. In few cases, contact person is another person from the main office bearers.

As regards female workers also, not less than 50 per cent workers are female workers. In case of NGOs running schools, the number of female workers far exceeds it. The situation is similar in districts of Ajmer, Alwar, Bikaner, Kota, Tonk, Dausa, Chittorgarh, Barmer etc. In case of Jaipur, it even exceeds 50 per cent limit.

Operational Area

In no case the area of operation is beyond Rajasthan state. Working area of NGO generally reflects the size of NGO i.e., the bigger the working area, the larger the size of that NGO with reference to number of workers. Approximately, 80 per cent NGOs are working only in rural areas, whereas 20 per cent carry out their activities in rural and urban areas both.

Similarly, 80–85 per cent of NGOs restrict their activities to one district and a few Panchayat Samitis in that district. Few NGOs confine their activities even in one Panchayat Samiti of the relevant district. Only about 15–20 per cent have working area in 3–5 districts and even more also and have networking with other NGOs. 'Networking programme' is a mutual relationship programme in which NGOs interact with each other. It may work for dissemination of information, exchange of technology, legal aspects, project preparation work on a 'give and take' basis. URMUL, Shanti Maitri Mission, Jagori, Proudh Shikshan Samiti of Bikaner, Seva Mandir, Astha, Jagaran, Prayas, Sahyog of Udaipur, CASA Udaipur, CECOECECON, CUTS, Chetna, RVHA, CARE, Sidart, The Rajasthan Hunger Project, DCNC, I-India, ARAVALI, State Resource Centre, Bhagirathi Foundation, Lapodia, Doosra Dashak, VIVIDHA, Mamta of Jaipur, UNNATTI and Divya Lok Sansthan of Jodhpur, Nehru Yuva Kendra in Barmer and other districts, Tarun Bharat Sangh of Alwar, Bhagirathi Foundation, Bharatiya Yuva Sansthan, Jan Morcha Rajasthan have networking relationship in many districts. Even agencies outside Rajasthan like Poverty Foundation California, Family Planning Association of India Bombay, C.I.S. Bombay, D.C.S. Bangalore, intersect worldwide, National Book Trust, New Delhi, G.S.S.S., Delhi, I.S.S New Delhi have linkages with NGOs in various districts.

As against all these networking relationships, NGOs of Sawai Madhopur, Jhalawar, Sikar and few other districts could not be found coordinating the network with NGOs.

Sources of Funds

Money makes the mare go. NGOs cannot go a long way only with membership fees and donation. Grants from national and international funding agencies are the lifeblood for NGOs for the efficient and meaningful impact of activities in the area of operation. It is generally seen that ministries of central government like Ministry of Empowerment and Social Justice or State Government Departments of Social Welfare, Zila Parishad, Women and Child Development Department are major source of funds for NGOs. International UN funding agencies like UNICEF, CARE, or Tata Trust, Bombay etc., also support NGOs for their projects. The main funding agencies from whom NGOs are receiving grant as listed by NGOs themselves are as under:

- *International Funding* Agencies like Poverty Foundation, California, T.D.H. Germany, K.K.S. Germany, UNICEF,

CARE, Hunger Project; Child Line India Foundation, ActionAid, UNFPA.

- *Central Government* Agencies like Ministry of Social Justice and Empowerment, Ministry of Forest and Environment, Ministry of Labour, Medical and Family Planning Department, New Delhi.
- *Central Agencies* like Central Social Welfare Board, Bharatiya Samajik Vigyan Anusandhan Parishad New Delhi, NABARD, SIDBI, CAPART, N.F.I Delhi, VANI New Delhi, I.S.S. New Delhi, BAIF, VHAI New Delhi,
- *State Government Departments* like District Industries Centre, Zila Parishad, Social Welfare Board, Social Welfare Department, Women and Child Development Department, Medical and Health Department, Municipal Councils, Labour Department, IGPRS and SIRD Jaipur,
- *Other Agencies* like CASA Udaipur, Seva Mandir Udaipur, CUTS Jaipur, PRIA New Delhi, Sri Ratan Tata Trust Bombay, Ahinsa Charitable Trust, Rajasthan Mahila Kalyan Mandal Ajmer, RVHA Jaipur, CECOEDECON Jaipur, Sambhav Ahmedabad, Chetna Sansthan Ahmedabad, T.B.S., RCDP Rajasthan, Nehru Yuva Kendra.

Donation, membership fees, subscriptions, school fees etc., have also been shown as other sources of funds by respective NGOs.

Problems and Challenges

NGOs were also asked to indicate their problems. Major problems given by them are as:

- Lack of financial resources by 80 per cent NGOs.
- Lack of infrastructure facilities.
- In 10 per cent cases, problem was that they had no building of their own.
- Others had difficulty in project preparation especially for foreign funding agencies.

- Moreover they told that big donor agency do not reach at village level.
- Government departments did not give grant timely.
- They could not get timely guidance from the funding and technical agencies also.
- Indifference of government officials towards NGOs treating them as inferior was also a problem faced by NGOs.
- Public was not in direct contact with the government officials, hence they could not feel the problems being faced in the field i.e., local situations.
- Elected representatives also did not favour NGOs at some places.

On the other side, NGOs as underlisted field problems and challenges during implementation of programmes:

- Illiteracy or lack of education among women.
- Lack of health awareness among women.
- Programme for Kishori Balikas is not given due priority.
- Problems of health services i.e., at the time of delivery of child.
- Lack of proper sanitation.
- Poverty.
- Unemployment.
- Absence of home industry in rural areas.
- Absence of training programmes for self-employment of women.
- Population pressure.
- Drinking water problem.
- Problem of electricity.
- Migration during drought.
- No school for child labourers.
- Lack of ashram for widows.

Experiences during Compilation of NGOs Research Directory: By the Research Team

- At the first step formats were sent by post to 1,545 NGOs working in 32 districts of Rajasthan, approximately 1,000 NGOs did not respond perhaps either their address had changed and letters were returned back to IDS-J, they might not be dealing with women and children or because they ignored to respond.
- Some of NGOs had stopped functioning or changed their office address. Hence, they could not be contacted.
- Though efforts were made to find out changed addresses of NGOs, but such cases were few in numbers.
- Some NGOs did not respond perhaps because they did not like to share their balance sheets and audited statements as informed by them.
- Since the directory has to include NGOs dealing with women and children, letters were sent to project directors, DWCD of all the 32 districts. DWCD Sikar and Jhunjhunu were kind enough to send such lists.
- Some NGOs told that they did not need any finances, since they had adequate funds. Hence they did not want inclusion of their names in aforesaid directory.
- Few NGOs do not want to include their details in directory. In their view it is not needed as they are popular enough in state, country and internationally.
- Some NGOs have their main office at other states, their branch office is operating at district level. The information could not be collected from such offices due to unavailability of full information at branch office.
- UNICEF provided funds by end of February 2005, whereas project work was started from January itself.

Gaps in Available Services Being Rendered for Children and Women

NGOs were asked to give suggestions for more effective implementation of women and child programmes. Some important suggestions quoted by them are as under:

For Women

- More programmes should be run for women and child development.
- Awareness generation for women especially for health should be prioritized.
- Skill development for occupation/self-employment should be emphasized.
- SHG formation should not only be restricted to thrift activity but for self-employment also.
- Programme of home industries by DIC may be run on PMRY pattern.
- Health services should reach in distant areas.
- Programmes for Kishori Balika should be separated from ICDS.
- Programmes should be run for women workers also.
- Dalit women should be covered specially.
- Widows' ashram should also be run along with some economically productive work like 'Lizzat Papad'.
- Removal of social evils and drug addiction should be dealt with specifically as a separate programme.
- Leadership development programme for elected women representatives should be organized on regular basis.
- Day care centres for elderly women may also be started.
- Rehabilitation of mentally challenged women is not being done properly.
- Programme for women of age group of 18–25 years should be run separately.

- Programmes for prevention of atrocities against women should be strengthened.
- Legal awareness programme for women should be started by a larger number of NGOs.

For Children

- Schools for child labourers should be opened.
- Creches for children of working women should be started as a programme.
- Bal Sanskar Kendra and Balwadi scheme should be introduced.
- Separate schools for orphan, viklang and footpath children should be started like ashram schools.
- Night schools should be run for child labourers.
- Bal Ashram should be started like widow homes.
- Awareness generation about child rights should be created.

Reorientation and Strengthening the Network on Women and Child Rights

To further strengthen the network the resource directory can help into a truly collaborative effort. This may be done by:

- Constant meetings with organizations listed in the directory on their activities and planning.
- Sending required information to all organizations.
- Sending a letter (quarterly) to organizations listed in the resource directory.
- The next step may be preparing a national resource directory. This resource directory will also be the basis for reviewing the services available to women and children on a national level, identifying regional variations and intake policies of organizations. This would help in advocating national policy level changes.

Government of India has included Child Rights in Tenth Five-Year Plan (2002–07) document also. Since 1990, special emphasis is being laid on education, health and nutrition of children. NGOs have also highlighted gaps for child rights, Kishori Girls, self-employment and training needs for women etc. Hence, capacity building of NGOs needing guidance for project preparation also needs to be facilitated. Dialogue at government level to develop government organization-NGO relationship to remove suspicion and ensure transparency in NGO working is also required to develop a healthy environment for effective working of NGOs in the field of development of women and children.

It is hoped that this assessment report and resource directory will serve as a valuable source of information to voluntary sector professionals and volunteers, government departments, corporates, journalists etc., who want to associate with the voluntary sector as well as public in general who wish to support this sector. This will help with advocating for better services for women and children in Rajasthan. The list given in the directory can be used as a resource base to initiate a process of dialogue between the needy, community and helplines to share the issues with a view to reach out to the needy women and children in the society. The resource directory is useful to all those interested in the well-being of women and children.

10 NGO Sector in India in the Era of Globalization and Economic Liberalization

D.N. Reddy

Pioneering Efforts

NGO sector in India is very vast and as complex as any sector. The structure is labyrinthine and the processes which govern the structure are numerous and hazy. To understand this sector, not many studies are available and those studies which exist do not give adequate information on some of the questions of a common person.

However, NGO sector in India is very vibrant and is recognized for its capacity, innovativeness and concern for the people. It has no doubt been able to carve a niche for itself in the democratic set-up of India, far surpassing the performance of the four pillars of democracy. Many a life, families, communities and sections of population have benefited from the role and performance of NGOs. NGOs today encompass every walk of life, and even peep into the personal ways of life. They have worked on different methodologies, from questioning to awareness to fighting for the projects and programmes. NGOs have implemented projects, demonstrated the efficacy of alternative methods of service delivery and in general have been able to provide comprehensive methodologies to the public domain.

NGOs in India have also been at the forefront of bringing in social change. Many villages today have benefited from the interventions of NGOs in terms of removing social barriers, and rigid social customs. Disadvantaged and poorer sections of the society across the country did mobilize themselves through self-help groups to improve their financial conditions. Awareness programmes by NGOs have increased pressure on government delivery services. NGOs have also facilitated the proper utilization of government welfare and development schemes. They have often influenced the formulation of schemes and also reorientation of some of the existing schemes and projects. NGOs have helped the media in highlighting socially perilous practises, exposed corruption and had targeted bureaucrats and politicians. They have lobbied with the parliament, government and political parties.

They have contributed to education and awareness of citizens on the role and responsibilities of individual citizens and democratic structures. Service delivery and education and awareness programmes have been core functions of NGOs. However, in times of emergencies and crises, NGOs have provided relief and rehabilitation. They helped individuals and communities on the periphery of government-led relief services. They have challenged the governments on rehabilitation and displacement. NGOs have established alternative models of service delivery, development and conservation of natural resources. Governments were forced to copy and/or follow some of these models. An acknowledgement of this work comes from the government whenever NGOs are appointed on advisory committees.

NGOs have done research projects, and have organized capacity building, training and education programmes in areas where universities and formal educational institutions had failed to focus upon. Today, many of the best research projects which influenced policy and social thinking have come from the NGO sector. The agenda of social change has been brought under the influence of NGO sector long time back. NGOs have been successful in highlighting some of the aspects of social change forgotten by other actors of social development. Political parties had to redesign their election agenda because of the diligent work of NGOs. NGOs have defied religious fundamentalism and diktats by paternalistic and dictatorial leaderships. They have brought out thousands of cases of atrocities and exploitation into the public domain. They had succeeded in stopping such exploitation in many cases, and had failed in taking up more cases. They had also prevented many more atrocities through education, campaigns, forcing the governments to work, create special institutions and influencing public opinion.

NGOs have worked on economics, sociology and politics of this country. They have often motivated communities to become pressure groups. NGOs have become a force to reckon with at the international level, often influencing public opinion, government policies, international treaties, events and consultations.

How Did they Do it?

NGOs did this by basically reaching out to the people, asking them, facilitating their participation and in general focusing on the issues and developing a thorough understanding of the situation. Work of the NGO sector and the success belongs to either individual NGOs, individuals behind such NGOs, a network of NGOs, or disparate attempts which cumulatively brought in the change. Together they undertook campaigns but worked individually in their respective geographical and thematic areas. Careful planning and development of vision, mission and goals qualify their work.

They mobilized funds from a variety of sources including individuals, trusts, charities, foundations, governments (Indian and foreign) and foreign non-governmental organizations. Their self-sustaining mechanisms, equally include an innovative range of methods, from publications to door-to-door collections. However, the bulk of funds are sourced from foreign aid, followed by government schemes and projects.

NGOs depended largely on their facilitation and grass-roots work and approach. They spent hours with the targeted people to bring them 'on board'. They used innovative techniques in this process. Today, a number of such methods have gained acceptance with the governments and other sections of the society.

Some of this work bordered on defying social customs, established norms and law. They used every democratic method. NGO sector has effectively utilized the judiciary and media to further the interests of the people. Public interest litigation has gained acceptance by the work of NGOs. High profile cases against self-interested corporate sector were also taken up by the NGOs. Some of the landmark judgments belong to the cases filed by NGOs. NGO personnel faced the wrath of governments and other 'self-interest' groups for their work and stand. A few have been killed, jailed and punished in various ways. But rarely they were rejected by the people.

What is the Motivation for Their Work?

Motivation for NGO work was basically from the individuals who were/are part of that particular NGO. These individuals had different reasons for their motivation to do such work. Some stood up because they were affected personally. Some responded to the 'inner' call, probably caused by education, seeing the suffering, psychology, and/or basic instincts. For many others, it was also a job, a source of employment and a way of life. People were also influenced by the work of other NGOs. Motivation also came from campaigns, experiences and the knowledge. Life and work of individuals such as Mahatma Gandhi, B.R. Ambedkar and many others was also one of the motivating factors.

Injustice, exploitation, irrelevant social customs and taboos had also been fulcrum of many NGO campaigns. Anti-people policies were able to bring in serious individuals to work on advocacy issues. Totalitarian behaviour of governments, unfair and illogical development projects also helped some of the NGOs to take up the work. Concern for children, women, poor people, and other disadvantaged sections of population can also be considered as part of this motivation.

NGO personnel come from different backgrounds, education and social strata. Illiterate individuals, victims of exploitation, dalits and other sections have started NGOs also.

Critical Look

NGO sector is increasingly being influenced systematically. Foreign funds are used to construct a particular agenda for the entire NGO sector. Networking campaigns are usually suspect because of the planning and the wide canvass. Quite a number of NGOs are purely money making/business organizations. NGOs in general lack democratic structures internally. Their office work is often not transparent. There are many instances where funds were misused, or diverted for wrong purposes. Government departments often find that they have been duped by 'suitcase' NGOs—an acronym for individuals who run NGOs in their suitcases. Many NGO failures in delivering the promised benefits to people were never documented, and brought into the public domain. Efficiency of work, and productivity is often low in NGO work. Like in government schemes, in many NGO projects, percolation of money to the targeted people is not even five per cent of the funds mobilized—most of it is spent on infrastructure, vehicles and other paraphernalia. The actual beneficiary may not get much.

NGOs are not subject to public accountability. Though legal accountability exists, it is marred by corruption and inadequate government regulations and regulatory structures. It is no surprise that many individuals have become millionaires by establishing NGOs. There is a change in composition of the NGO sector over the years. There are now more professionals than volunteers. Domination of few castes and classes can be seen in the NGO leadership. Articulation capacities still remain with the individuals who belong to erstwhile dominant castes and classes. There are invisible and secret networks within the sector, which perpetuate the very norms against which NGO sector is supposed to be championing.

NGOs do not often take responsibility of the people's aspirations, which they helped in raising. Awareness programmes without concurrent and/or follow up programmes end in disillusionment at best, or loss of faith in all social and democratic institutions. There have been instances where NGOs have abandoned projects midway, for mere financial reasons. Networks have often failed in delivering the objectives formulated by themselves. Most have been marred by individual avarice, egos and corruption. Many networks do exist to serve the self-interest of a particular NGO(s) or individual(s). Individuals in the garb of NGOs exploited vulnerable sections, such as women, illiterates and others. Individuals in the NGO sector, effectively shielding themselves from law and other social mechanisms, have committed serious crimes. Some NGOs have also furthered their narrow interests (for getting funds) by appearing to work with Left Movements and intellectuals, though the movements did not get any benefit out of such alliances. NGOs have often been used to perpetuate social exploitation and rigid customs. Individuals have used the ladder of NGOs to improve their social and financial position. Some used it to further their individual careers.

Globalization and Economic Liberalization Context

NGO sector today is a *sine qua non* of any democracy. Any wishful thinking would easily endorse the NGO sector. NGO sector is as complex as the society it serves. It has become part and parcel of the public institutional structure. The Earth Summit of 1992 in Rio de Janeiro was a watershed in raising the international position of the NGO sector. After this event, NGO sector was recognized by the United Nations and has been given official participative position, almost on par with the governments. As United Nations is known to be on other side of globalization and economic liberalization (GEL) principally being pushed by developed countries, Brettonwood Institutions and multinational corporations. Probably, recognition of NGO sector was probably to counter these forces at the international level. However, this on hindsight shows that, was probably a response to the growth of globalization and economic liberalization.

In any case, it is now established that NGO sector in India is linked very strongly with the forces of change based abroad, even before the era of GEL. These links were used, misused and exploited variously. Positively, these links helped in bringing in fresh development and social perspectives, technologies and methodologies, reiteration of confidence and strength in traditional systems of living and livelihoods. However, the suspicion over the motives of foreign funding remains. These became accentuated in the last four to five years, as the GEL process gained momentum.

GEL process has invariably been knocking off traditional and conventional methods of governance, trade and business and has been impacting upon a number of sections of the society negatively. This process has been enabled by huge grants and loans to the governments, semi-government institutions and trade. It is no wonder funds to NGOs might also have roots in such process, or game plan.

To establish this fact, or disprove this, a proper and thorough analysis of NGO sector is needed. The debate over funds to the Asian Social Forum in Hyderabad in January, 2003 brings out the need to do so. Foreign funds are suspected for their objectives and motivation. However, it is also a fact that social change, the kind of social change espoused by NGOs, does have few takers within India. Status quo is what is desired by upper and middle class sections of the society, who have the money. They would not be part of any campaigns which would change such a 'cosy' situation. In fact, this is the reason why political parties, and other political movements, have to use coercion tactics to get finances for their activities. NGOs, being small, would not be able to adopt such methods. Often these methods delay the implementation of projects. This is not to say that foreign funds alone would help in social change. In general, the support for NGOs and for the kind of work they do is very minimal internally.

Now, the obvious question is why people and institutions abroad are interested in sending funds for social change in India. Apparently, there is no single reason for such motivation—it could be charity, fear of god, sympathy, policy, philosophy, social structure, etc. Cumulatively, foreign funds today constitute a major source for the NGO sector, government, political movements and business.

GEL has its direct impact on 'independent' foreign funding. It is now an established fact that foreign funds for NGOs in Andhra Pradesh gradually decreased parallel to the growth of World Bank funding and the WB-led reform programme in Andhra Pradesh. Most of the development and service delivery NGOs invariably had to seek funds from World Bank-funded projects and programmes.

In fact, these projects basically administered by the state government mirror the jargon, vocabulary, planning, methodologies and tools employed by the NGOs. Most NGOs saw this as an opportunity to expand their area of work and results. However, experience of NGOs with these projects proved otherwise. Each of the projects where NGOs partnered with the government had the hidden agenda of furthering GEL objectives. Being small and resource dependent, many small NGOs succumbed to the pressure and were reduced to doing 'contract' jobs for the government. Thus, the state legitimized its agenda of GEL by 'partnering' with NGOs. Of course, there are few NGOs who clearly tow GEL philosophy and act as agents of the government. Thus, the agents of change for welfare of the people are now reduced to carrying the change dictated by GEL forces.

In addition, genuine NGOs are now forced to compete with NGOs started by contractors, political leaders, former bureaucrats and business people. These NGOs, often derisively called as government-organized NGOs (GONGOs) have achieved more visibility because of their participation in the high profile projects of the government. One can easily detect the difference between such NGOs and the genuine, grass-roots work based NGOs. Personnel of these NGOs are high-heeled, hobnob with the officials, comfortable in the environs of five-star hotels, work through consultants, have corporate-style offices and quite comfortable with English language and official communications.

In any case, genuine NGOs have been successful in keeping up the fight against GEL at the global level, and have been able to take the fight to the 'subjects' of developed country regimes. People in developed countries were often influenced, and thus their government policies, by successful NGO campaigns and sympathetic networks across the world. A good example would be the WTO agreements. NGOs have been able to force the governments to negotiate and renegotiate terms and conditionalities in various agreements (example: TRIPS) under the ambit of WTO. But for NGOs, many government would have succumbed to the pressures generated by MNCs and the ruling classes of the developed countries.

Developing Synergies within the Civil Society

In general, people of Andhra Pradesh have been facing the brunt of GEL-induced reforms brought in under the overall framework of Vision 2020. Vision 2020 is the blue print brought about by the TDP government. Presently, no section of the population has remained untouched by these changes. Resultantly, poor people and weaker sections of the population have been suffering enormously. Government has been following the agenda of privatization of resources, export-led growth, urban-suited infrastructure development and consolidation of trade, business and professions. The agenda is clearly in favour of multinational corporations and everything espoused by them.

In this regard, it is important to build synergy within the civil society of Andhra Pradesh, which includes development NGOs, political and social movements, associations and organizations committed to community development. Often political and social movements are suspicious about the motivations of NGOs, principally because of the funds linkage. These movements feel that NGOs are tools of GEL process, and are employed by the state to legitimize the agenda of GEL. While this is true in a limited sense, NGOs cannot be seen as a singular entity. Like the society in which they are working, NGOs come in all colours, shapes and principles. A sweeping generalization would not be able to stick to the entire sector. Further, NGO sector cannot be looked or analyzed in isolation.

Secondly, the character of NGO has always been to work within the legal framework, often questioning and changing the framework. This is the strength of the NGOs, which are small and individualistic. However, this characteristic is very effective in delivering the 'goods'. Thirdly, a good network of NGOs would be able to strategize the campaign against a government order or move, which is against the interests of the people. NGOs have the reach to information and would also be able to influence the bureaucracy and policymakers to include people's interests. This might not be the best way, but this also a method. There are several instances when government had to withdraw/rescind a particular order because of pressure from NGOs.

Most of the personnel in the NGOs belong to the middle class (somebody might reach it, once he/she starts getting salary and/or funding). A worker in the smallest NGO, or an animator, would also be a middle class person in a village. Synergy between NGOs and political movements would mean achieving the support of middle class in aligning with the struggles of the poor people. Uncluttered information, devoid of ideologies, is the strength of the NGO sector's efforts on many of the issues, such as watershed development, forest conservation, water conservation, agriculture and farmer's issues, rights for tribals, dalits, women, children, and sustainable livelihoods for traditional professions.

A general complaint of the people's movements is that NGOs are helping in 'dissipating' the anger of the people by bringing in sops as part of the government-partnered programmes. There are two aspects which are worth noting. One, anger dissipation is done by various setups variously, especially political parties, media and caste and class associations. In fact, political parties are very effective in channelizing this anger into purposes of their own. An individual NGO is pretty small compared to these efforts. The biggest NGOs might work in 15 villages (even if they claim to be working in different districts and mandals). Within the village, their target group is much less. Secondly, people are not always ready for struggles, especially the poor. They would like to exhaust all options before they get prepared for the struggles. Interim programmes of awareness by the NGOs would largely help the cause of the people. Mahatma Gandhi had effectively used this strategy off and on in the Independence struggle.

NGOs in general encourage people to become independent, while political movements seek to link them up with government. Self-help movement was started by NGOs and has been quite successful in lifting many families and individuals (especially women) to become independent and have sustainable livelihood programme. It is their belief that economic independence frees them from oppressive social frameworks and bondage. Education helps in the growth of the individuals self and confidence. NGOs aim for attitudinal change in the people and probably no more.

Most of them do not go beyond this agenda. However, there have been efforts by individuals and NGOs to fight for the rights of communities (dalits, Adivasis, SCs and STs). It has to be acknowledged that the 'rights' agenda has been brought on to the mainstream socio-political agenda only after it was taken up by the NGOs, though the Left movements have been espousing it for a long time.

As somebody said: "When we consider people's participation as the lifeline of development process, persons irrespective of the roles they play, should be familiar with ethos, strengths, weaknesses, limitations and needs of the poor and rural communities." NGO sector, as a tool and a mechanism, helps in better understanding of these characteristics of the communities. Today, NGOs collaborate with universities and social scientists in social science research, which brings out the needs and necessities of the people. In the event of failure of universities, media, judiciary and public institutions, NGOs offer the alternatives with a rare amalgamation of skills, expertise, concern, commitment and grass-roots linkages.

Conclusion

People's movements have to understand NGO sector more thoroughly and analyze its strengths and weaknesses. Lampooning the entire sector, with a few corrupt NGOs, would not help the cause of the people, who have benefited substantially from the programmes and projects of the NGOs. NGO sector is a legitimate, legal tool which can bring in unbelievable strengths to the people's movements in many ways, principally by transferring information alone across the world. In fact, today anti-globalization campaign is being championed by NGOs far beyond their individual capacities simply through sharing information and skills. Afraid of this combined strength, MNCs and governments have been initiating a number of measures to shut them out.

11 Role of Non-Governmental Organizations in Tribal Development

An Overview

Jadi Musalaiah

The non-governmental or the voluntary organizations have been playing a crucial role in all the weaker socio-economic spheres, including that of the tribal peoples in India. At one level, they can be termed as the 'means' by which the nation makes optimum use of its human resources. However, the mushrooming of voluntary organizations working in the field of rural development in recent years has generated widespread debate about their role, structure, programmes and performance.

A unique feature of voluntary organizations is that they stimulate voluntary action among the target community and involve the progressive elements of that community. In the present context of human resource development, voluntary organizations, in their functioning, have demonstrated the freedom and flexibility of working with a personal touch, a capacity for initiative and experimentation with novel programmes. Thus, voluntary organizations exercise full freedom in selecting localities for programme implementation and are free of bureaucratic hassles.

In the Indian context, the attributes of a tribe are that they live in relative isolation of hills and covered forests, and often in geographical areas accessible to the mainstream population. Tribes generally are groups without a written letter or script. Their sense of history is shallow or mixed with mythology, and in terms of their cultural ethos, language, customs, institutions and beliefs, they stand out from other sections of society.

In India, tribes have different names such as Vanyajati, Vanavasi, Pahariya, Adimajati, Janajati, Anusuchit Jati and scheduled tribes—all of which mean the 'aboriginal'. India stands second in terms of tribal population after Africa in the world. According to the 2001 Census, the total population of the tribals is 84.2 million, and accounts for 8.2 per cent of the country's population. There are about 689 scheduled tribes speaking about 105 languages and 225 subsidiary languages. They have traditionally lived in about 15 per cent of the nation's geographical area, mainly forests, hills and the undulating inaccessible terrains in plateau areas that are rich in natural resources. They have lived mostly as isolated entities for centuries together and this explains their politico-socio-economic backwardness.

However, we have to acknowledge that even before the freedom struggle, a few voluntary organizations were active in the sphere of tribal welfare. They also played a significant role in the field of rural development and nation building and continued to do so. Many great personalities took initiatives to form such organizations, which at present, are performing a key role at the grass-roots level in implementing various developmental works. Until such time that a genuinely democratic machinery of governance evolves, there will remain a strong urge for voluntary organizations to play a mediating role between the state and the people.

As early as 1871, the Bhil Seva Mandal came up in Gujarat. At that time, A.V. Thakkar was the moving spirit behind voluntary organizations committed to tribal development. By the time India got independence, he could establish more than 20 voluntary institutions in different parts of the country. Some other leaders in the

Indian National Congress were also involved in tribal development activities. Rajendra Prasad's Bharatiya Adim Jati Sevak Sangh helped a lot in shaping the tribal policy when the Indian Constitution was in the drafting stage.

Various approaches have been evolved in the country in the domain of tribal affairs; prominent among them are the voluntary agency approach, the political approach and the anthropological approach. These three approaches find support in three important policies: (1) Policy of Isolation (2) Policy of Assimilation and (3) Policy of Integration.

After independence, the policy of integration was found to be the most suitable one. Also, Nehru's concept of tribal integration was reflected in the successive five-year plans. The policy of integration is the outcome of serious research activities undertaken by many social anthropologists in India. Its main objective is 'social integration and cultural assimilation'.

It was in the Fifth Five-Year Plan that the tribal sub-plan (TSP) approach was adopted. In order to fulfil the sub-plan objectives nearly 198 ITDAs and 257 MADA pocket, 78 clusters and 75 micro projects for primitive tribal groups (PTGs) were set up all over the country. Consequently, various strategies came into being. With the passage of time, it has widely been noted that the programmes and activities related to tribal development cannot be implemented by the governments alone. Thus, the significance of participation of the community and the role of voluntary organizations/NGOs was realized in this all-important sphere.

Voluntary Organizations are Necessary

(a) to supplement government efforts in such fields where the administrative machinery has no reach.

(b) and to fight against policies and actions which encourage exploitation of the helpless groups and render help to such social groups, including the tribal groups, to stand on their own feet to protect their ways of living and lifestyles.

A voluntary organization can easily adapt itself to the needs of the people. A sensitive worker can assess each specific situation with sympathy and personal care. Thus, the gulf that arises between what should be done and what is being done as a result of somewhat inflexible operation of the administrative apparatus can be bridged.

Objectives of NGOs/Voluntary Organizations

Whatever the nature of NGOs/voluntary organizations may be, they play a key role in the upliftment of the weaker sections of society. The objectives of voluntary or non-governmental agencies include some or all of the following:

(i) To create an awareness regarding participation in socio-economic development.
(ii) To create an able and efficient local leadership.
(iii) To assist in the planned efforts to create socio-economic infrastructural facilities.
(iv) To facilitate the process of expanding employment opportunities.
(v) To induce appropriate persons to set up small-scale productions and
(vi) To make the tribals give up the pre-agricultural technology and seek better education.

Role of NGOs/Voluntary Organizations

NGOs/voluntary organizations have a long history of active involvement in the promotion of human welfare and development. They come up with a mission to serve a human cause, spontaneously—voluntarily and without any compulsion or control, to fulfil certain needs of specific groups of people. These organizations are flexible and possess the virtue of humanitarian service with concern. Voluntary action is the soul of social action as this medium secures active involvement of the people from policy making to implementation of programmes. Their activities cover a diverse range of functions in the welfare sector. The programmes of voluntary organizations are strictly service-oriented, professional in nature and specialized in functions.

The essential feature of voluntary action is that it fixes the problem. It starts to not only to solve a problem but also to prevent the occurrence of it. Voluntary action, thus, ultimately aims at creating a situation conducive to the development of potentialities in individuals, groups and communities so they can find solutions to their problems and realize their ultimate goals.

Regarding the role and nature of voluntary organizations, there appear to be two different views. Some are happy with the functioning of such organizations and plead for their increasing role. According to them, these organizations should be given ample scope to serve people. For, the government agencies crippled as they are with bureaucratic complications and rigidity, have failed to work satisfactorily. Others hold that it is undesirable to give undue importance and authority to voluntary agencies as there is a great possibility of institutionalizing the chances.

In this context, the suggestion is that the voluntary organizations should be given ample scope to work in collaboration and cooperation with the government agencies and subject to strict government scrutiny and monitoring. The need for involving the NGOs in rural development was highlighted and acknowledged by various official committees set up by the Government of India. One of these was the Balwant Rai Mehta Committee (1957) which in its report emphasized that during the implementation of community development schemes more and more emphasis should be laid on NGO's/VOs. The Dhebar Commission in its report on the scheduled areas and scheduled tribes opined that the principle of active and purposeful participation of people at all levels could best be served by assigning an important role to non-official organizations. It is necessary in any democratic framework to take up some of the nation-building activities under non-official auspices.

The report of the committee on Panchayat Raj Institutions (1973) appreciated the role of voluntary organizations in the development of rural and interior areas. The committee reiterated that these organizations could be particularly involved in conceiving projects and schemes. They can be of great help in creating strong public opinion in support of measures of social change. The Sivaraman Committee set up by the Government of India also recommended involvement of voluntary organizations in planning and implementation of the integrated rural development programmes. Thus, there exists a widespread agreement among all the concerned that voluntary organizations have an important role to play in the overall development of the rural areas.

Grant-in-Aid to Voluntary Organizations for the Welfare of the Scheduled Tribes

The Ministry of Tribal Affairs is the key governmental agency with respect to the welfare and development of the tribal peoples all over the country. It is the responsibility of the ministry to reach the target groups, particularly the tribals living in remote and inaccessible areas. The objective is to bring them into the mainstream of development by assisting them to overcome their social, psychological and educational backwardness. Capacity building is the key factor here. Such training would equip them to employ their capabilities to their fullest potential thereby reducing their reliance on others and achieving self-sustenance to the maximum extent possible—which is the ultimate goal of the government.

The NGOs supplement the efforts of the state in ensuring that the benefits reach the maximum number of people. In certain cases, voluntary organizations are in a better position to implement the governmental schemes in a more efficient manner than the administrative machinery. This is primarily attributable to the highly committed and dedicated human resources that are available with the voluntary organizations.

The role of NGOs was in the reckoning since the First Five-Year Plan. Many organizations have done a commendable job in tribal areas and are still active. Since the last two decades, there has been an exponential growth in the number of NGO/VOs approaching the ministry of tribal affairs for financial assistance.

It has been felt that along with few very dedicated and committed voluntary organizations/non-governmental organizations a large number of other organizations have also come up that want to grab public funds for their narrow and selfish interests. The ministry would take all the possible steps to curb the entry of such voluntary organizations/non-governmental organizations in the field of tribal welfare.

The Ministry of Tribal Affairs feels that some organizations solely depend on aid from the government. This situation has to change. The voluntary organizations should aim to expand their effort on the support from the government and thereafter establish other support systems that could free them from financial constraints.

It should be the intention of the organizations to obtain support of other sources for their work. This can happen after they establish themselves with the support of the government and prove their usefulness to society at large. If the impression that NGOs can support themselves financially gains ground, then the support of corporate houses and even the community would follow as a natural consequence. Contribution, both in kind and cash, would come easily once their credentials are firmly established. Additional resources, if necessary, could also be mobilized.

Voluntary organizations should make all possible efforts to involve the community in their work. Community participation helps in building confidence among the people and in providing feedback for further improvement and reorientation of the programmes. Thus, the long-term interests of the tribal communities can be served.

The Ministry of Tribal Affairs endeavours to provide full advantage of all schemes to the non-governmental organizations/voluntary organizations that have absolute credentials in the field of tribal welfare. It also wants to promote new groups with brilliant ideas and new strategies for the speedy development of the targeted people.

It has been the constant endeavour of the ministry to identify the voluntary organizations/non-governmental organizations which have an all India character and are known for their selfless service and facilitate them with some preferential treatment with regard to sanction of new proposals and relaxation of certain norms and conditions relating to release of annual grants. In this direction, the ministry has identified a few such organizations and categorized them as "Established Voluntaries Agencies (EVAs)"

The following organizations have been identified as the EVAs by the ministry:

1. Ram Krishna Mission and its affiliated organizations.
2. Akhil Bharatiya Banavasi Kalyan Ashram.
3. Bharat Sevashram Sangh and its affiliates.
4. Bharatiya Adim Jati Sevak Sangh.
5. Seva Bharati and its affiliated organizations.
6. Vidya Bharati and its affiliated organizations.
7. Swami Vivekanand Youth Movement.

Schemes in the Voluntary Sector

There are three ongoing schemes with the ministry, which are open to participation of the voluntary and non-governmental organizations. The schemes are:

Grant-in-aid to voluntary organizations working for welfare of scheduled tribes (GVWST).

Educational complex in low literacy pockets for the development of women's literacy in tribal areas (ECLP), Vocational training centres (VTC).

In addition to the said schemes, the ministry has an exclusive programme for non-governmental organizations with regard to the development of primitive tribal groups (PTGs).

Scheme of Grant-in-Aid to Voluntary Organizations Working for the Welfare of the Scheduled Tribes (GVWST)

The scheme is under implementation since 1953–54.

Objective

The prime objective of the scheme is to provide for an overall improvement and development of the target group i.e., the scheduled tribes through voluntary efforts in the fields of education, health and sanitation, environment, drinking water and legal services as well as the need-based socio-economic upliftment efforts. It also supports other relevant activities deemed appropriate and having a direct impact on the target group.

Salient Features

The grants are provided to the non-governmental organizations on their application in prescribed formats, in the form of supporting projects that meet the objectives of the scheme.

The NGOs are required to maintain separate accounts in respect of the grants released to them, which are open for inspection by all appropriate officers/agencies of the government. The NGO is also required to maintain separate accounts of Grant-in-Aid audited by the government auditor or a registered chartered accountant and submit complete set of copies of audited statement of accounts as prescribed by the ministry.

The grants are generally made in two instalments every year subject to satisfactory performance of the NGO.

Activities of the NGOs are monitored as per the established provisions of the financial rules besides field inspection by the ministry or the state government officials or by any other agency designated by the ministry.

Funding Pattern

The fund is generally granted to the extent of 100 per cent directly to the non-governmental organizations working in the scheduled areas on the recommendations of the state governments and the union territories. The non-governmental organizations are supported to the extent of 90 per cent of the project cost for projects in areas other than scheduled areas. However, the Ministry of Tribal Affairs has the discretion to assist even upto hundred per cent.

Schemes of Educational Complex in Low Literacy Pockets

The scheme was introduced in 1993–94 in 136 districts with less than 10 per cent literacy rate among tribal women. It is being implemented through:

(i) Non-governmental organizations
(ii) Institutions set up by the government as autonomous bodies, and
(iii) Registered cooperative societies.

Objectives

The primary objective of the scheme is the promotion of education among tribal girls in the targeted districts of the country. The secondary objective is to improve the socio-economic status of the economically backwards and the illiterate tribal masses.

Coverage

The scheme covers 136 districts with less than 10 per cent literacy among ST women spread over 14 states namely Andhra Pradesh, Bihar, Chattisgarh, Gujarat, Jharkhand, Madhya Pradesh, Orissa, Rajasthan, Tamil Nadu, Uttar Pradesh, Uttaranchal and West Bengal.

Procedure for Release of Grant-in-Aid and Funding Pattern

(a) The extent of assistance under the scheme would be 100 per cent in all cases.

(b) In the event of the Ministry of Welfare itself executing any element of the programme i.e., engagement of consultants, for project formulation, monitoring and evaluation, as well as expenses towards cost of training of NGO functionaries, etc., full cost shall be borne from the budgetary provision of the scheme.

(c) Under the programme, while predefined cost heads are stipulated at the project formulation stage, each implementing agency shall submit a detailed project proposal clearly bringing out the programme modalities and individual expenditure heads. Ministry of Welfare while approving the project shall indicate the extent of support to the project as a whole as well as to each component of the project against which re-appropriation to the extent 20 per cent of the total grant shall be permissible.

Salient Feature

Educational complexes can be set up in rural areas in the notified districts and can have classes upto V with provision for upgradation up to Class XII provided they have sufficient accommodation for classrooms, hostels, kitchen, garden and for sporting facilities.

These educational complexes impart not only formal education to tribal girls but also train students in agriculture, animal husbandry and other vocations and crafts as to make them skilled for leading a better life.

The teaching from classes I to III is imparted in tribal dialects of the area and women with proficiency in tribal dialect are engaged as teachers.

The strength of students for each class is fixed at 30, however a maximum of 10 more students, if available, in the locality are admitted as day scholars.

Performance of the Schemes

Grant-in-aid to Voluntary Working for the Welfare of Scheduled Tribes

(Rs in crore)

Year	*Allocation*	*Expenditure*	*NGO assisted*
1997–98	10.00	7.09	113
1998–99	20.00	11.31	190
1999–2000	28.00	15.25	140
2000–2001	28.00	22.00	228
2001–2002	27.00	25.00	110

Educational Development of ST Women

(Rs in crore)

Year	*Allocation*	*Expenditure*	*NGO assisted*
1997–98	4.00	2.20	54
1998–99	7.00	3.30	74
1999–2000	9.00	1.84	86
2000–2001	5.40	1.02	24
2001–2002	7.00	2.66	16

Vocational Training Centres in Tribal Area

(Rs in crore)

Year	*Allocation*	*Expenditure*	*NGO assisted*
1998–99	0.20	0.20	5
1999–2000	0.50	0.75	14
2000–2001	05.40	0.83	8
2001–2002	5.50	3.03	3

Establishment of Ashram Schools

The Ashram schools have played an important role in raising the literacy levels of the scheduled tribes. They provide the necessary environment conductive to learning. The schedule is in operation since 1990–91.

Construction of Girls' Hostel for Scheduled Tribes

The main objective of the scheme is to ensure adequate enrolment of scheduled tribe girls in educational institutions, particularly at the school stage. The scheme of girls' hostels for scheduled tribes has been in operation since the Third Five-Year Plan.

Construction of Boys' Hostel for Scheduled Tribes

The main objective of the scheme is to ensure adequate enrolment of scheduled tribe boys in educational institutions, particularly, at the high school level. The scheme of boys' hostel for scheduled tribes has been in operation since 1989–90 under the centrally-sponsored scheme of establishment of boys' hostel in tribal sub-plan areas.

Schemes for Primitive Tribal Groups (PTGs)

Objective

There are certain tribal communities that are having low levels of literacy, declining or stagnant population, and pre-agriculture level of technology and are economically backward. There are 75 such groups in 15 states/UTs that have been identified and categorized as the Primitive Tribal Groups (PTGs). Each of these groups is small in number, differentially developed with respect to one another, of remote habitat with poor administrative and infrastructure back up. Therefore, they are in urgent need of support from the government as well as the non-government agencies. Their protection and development at par with other tribal groups has to be accorded utmost priority.

The problems and needs of PTGs are quite different from other scheduled tribes. Since they constitute the most vulnerable among tribal groups, states/UTs have been requested to allocate requisite funds and plan special schemes for their socio-economic development. However, there are areas/activities, which though very crucial for the survival, protection and development of PTGs, are not specifically catered to by any existing scheme. Funds under this scheme should be used for such activities.

Scope

Such provisions/activities should not be identified only at the central level as they may differ from state to state and within a state from project to project (ITDA). However, funds under the scheme could be used for helping the beneficiaries of the project to cope with extremely adverse situations that threaten their very survival and protect them against various forms of exploitation thereby bringing them to a stage from where they can demand and receive specific assets and services. The activities under the scheme may include measures such as awareness generation and confidence-building, training for skill development of tribal youth, self-help groups and provision of services/inputs not covered by any existing scheme. In terms of beneficiaries, the scheme can cover maximum number of the PTGs.

Implementing Agency

The scheme will be implemented through Integrated Tribal Development Projects (ITDP)/Integrated Tribal Development Agencies (ITDAs), Tribal Research Institutes (TRI) and non-governmental organizations having requisite skills and determination. The state government concerned will be responsible for proper execution, implementation, supervision and coordination of the scheme, including selection of NGOs.

Terms and Conditions

1. The financial assistance as provided under the scheme should be utilized for the purpose it has been sanctioned and for the welfare of the members of the primitive tribal groups.
2. The financial assistance given to ITDPs/ITDAs and TRIs would deemed to be given to the state governments concerned and rules and regulations governing the grant-in-aid to states/UTs will apply to them.

3. The implementing agency shall allow the representative of the Ministry of Tribal Affairs or the state government to monitor or evaluate the actual working of the scheme.
4. The private agencies (NGOs) shall furnish a certificate to the effect that they accept the grant sanctioned to them subject to terms and conditions laid down by the Tribal Affairs Ministry. They should also furnish a bond with two sureties in the name of the competent authority signed by an office bearer duly authorized by the board of directors of the agency for the actual implementation of the scheme and submit accounts of the grant sanctioned by the ministry.

Vocational Training Centres

Objectives

There is a great need for vocational training centres in tribal areas where the left wing extremism is on the rise. Large-scale unemployment has been stoking rebellious tendencies among the tribal youth in such areas. The extremism is manifestation of frustration and lack of faith in the present pattern of development. It is necessary that both the state and central governments should make efforts to wean away the tribal youth from disruptive activities. Establishing vocational training institutes and creating a wide range of employment opportunities can be the way forward.

Non-governmental organizations shall meet the following requirements:

1. It is a registered body under an appropriate act so that it gets a corporate status. A legal personality and a group liability have to be established for its activities.
2. It has an appropriate administrative structure and a duly constituted managing/executive committee.
3. The aims and objects of the organizations and programmes in fulfilment of those aims and objects are clearly laid down; and
4. The organization is initiated and governed by its own members on democratic principles without any external control.

Procedure for Release of Grant-in-Aid

(a) Under the scheme, 100 per cent central assistance will be given to states/UTs/NGOs for setting up and running of vocational training centres.

(b) In the event of ministry of welfare itself executing any element of the programme i.e., engagement of consultants for project formulation, monitoring and evaluation as well as expenses towards cost of training of NGO functionaries etc., full cost shall be borne from the budgetary provision of the scheme.

(c) Under the programme while no predefined cost heads shall be stipulated at the project formulation stage, each implementing agency shall submit a detailed project proposal clearly bringing out the programme modalities and individual expenditure heads. Ministry of Welfare while approving the projects shall indicate the extent of support to the project as a whole as well as to each component of the project against which re-appropriation to the extent of 20 per cent of the total grant shall be permitted.

Conclusion

In India, we have a pluralistic society as opposed to a monolithic culture. The voluntary organizations cater to the needs of our cultural plurality. If we are to avoid concentration of power in the hands of a few, we must retain this multi-ethnic character of a free society and make full use of it. Voluntary organizations can serve as 'power breakers'. There is a need for wide decentralization of power, within the government from the national to the state level and then on to the local bodies, and also in ceding necessary powers to the voluntary organizations. Voluntary action in a society, partly within the areas of the state, helps achieve this objective of decentralization besides encouraging 'participatory' development.

Voluntary organizations provide an appropriate forum to those who wish to work for bringing about a change in society, but not necessarily through politics and political or governmental institutions. Efforts should be made to prepare people for a new kind of society through voluntary work. For instance, education is a state subject. The government runs educational institutions. However, alongside the state institutions, there could be services managed by voluntary organizations too. When the state's resources are limited, voluntary action would bring forth additional resources and cover the areas hitherto uncovered by the state. In view of their flexibility in operation, experimentation and innovation, pioneering spirit and other such qualities, voluntary organizations can continue to work for better standards, better methods and better forms of organization. They can also go in search of new needs, work in new areas, unveil and combat social evils and give priority to needs that are yet to get consideration.

However, there is another side to this debate. There is an argument that at the empirical-existential level voluntary agencies are nothing but the stooges of the ruling elite and the corporate sector, mainly of the capital finance variety. In this new role, voluntary organizations have created a crisis that begs a comprehensive solution. To what extent do the NGOs retain their commitment to the cause of the development of the tribals? Do they set a pattern for the government to emulate? The reality is altogether different. The combine of the government sanctions and the multinational agencies, in the form of corporate sector is all out to create a class of people to be exploited for sectarian interests. Is it possible for the NGOs to experiment and create new areas of work without the approval and consent of the funding body or agency, which in most cases is the government? In fact, the voluntary organizations are at the receiving end. Theoretically, the NGOs may vouch for their political neutrality, but in their day-to-day working, they are compelled to act as per the strategy and the line of approach put forth by the government or the funding agency whether domestic or foreign.

However, given the circumstances in terms of administrative or governmental reach, especially in the implementation of welfare schemes for the tribal peoples, we for once cannot deny the positive role of the non-governmental organizations. There are many areas yet to blink the state's radar. They are either very remote or inaccessible. In such a situation, the concerned and committed civil society groups have no other alternative but voluntary approach. The role of NGOs in the fields of education, health, sanitation, housing and particularly agriculture has not been a wide ranging one. We shall hope they would expand their area of action.

References

Dhebar, Commission Report on Scheduled Areas and Scheduled Tribes, Delhi, 1961.

Dude, S.C., *Approaches to Tribal Problems in India*, Kitab Mahal, Allahabad, 1968.

Franda, Marcus, *Voluntary Associations and Local Development in India: The Janta Phase*, New Delhi, Young Asia Publications, 1983.

Ghurye, G.S., *The Scheduled Tribes*, 2nd Edition, 1958.

Gore, M.S., Relative Roles of State and Voluntary Agencies in the Organisation of Social Services, Proceedings of the seminar on 'So Administration in Developing Countries', New Delhi, India International Centre, New Delhi, 1964.

Kulkarni, V.M., *Voluntary Action in a Developing Society*, New Delhi, Indian Institute of Public Administration, 1969.

Methe, D.R., "Legal Protection to Tribals and Tribal Development: A New Deal for Tribals and Tribal Development" in S.G. Deogaonkar (ed.), *Problems of Development of Tribal Areas*, 1980.

Shah, Ghanshyam and Chaturvedi, H.R., *Gandhian Approach to Rural Development: The Valid Experiment*, Delhi, Ajanta Book International, 1983.

Verghese, B.G., "Voluntary Action: A New Mission for the New Missionaries", *Voluntary Action*, XIV: 1, January-October, 1977.

Verrier, Elwin, *A New Deal for Tribal India*, 1963.

Windey, M.A., "A Rural Reconstruction Movement in India", *Voluntary Action*, XVIII: 3–4, March-April, 1976.

12 Role of NGOs in Empowerment of Women

A Study of Self-Help Groups

K. Padmavathi

In the last one and a half decade there has been a great deal of interest in the Indian voluntary organisation sector and its possible role in development. The attention, which these relatively small interventions in civil society have got, it is symptomatic of the complexity of development problems, compulsions of political economy and the centrality of the concern of reaching out to the poor. The non-governmental organizations (NGOs) are a relatively new phenomenon. Organizations today, whether voluntary or government, are an accepted fact of life. Individuals are surrounded by organizations all through their lives, whether they like them or not. The term organization includes a galaxy of institutions, such as hospitals, schools, factories, offices, armed forces and so on. Organizations of one type or another are indispensable to contemporary political realities. The NGOs are groups of persons organized on the basis of voluntary membership without state control, for the furtherance of some common interests of citizens.

Generally, voluntary organizations and NGOs are treated as one and the same. This is not true. All NGOs are not necessarily voluntary. Voluntary organizations are spontaneous in their origin whereas NGOs may also be government sponsored.

Generally, NGOs follow four clear-cut strategies. These are: simple charity, supplementing welfarism of the state, encouraging people's participation and implementing programmes launched by the government for the larger benefit of the community, involving people in programme planning, raising resources, implementing activities and sharing fruits of development and conscience-instilling and organizing people, enabling them to demand and undertake planning and implementation of development programmes beneficial to them.[1]

NGOs are a part of civil society. NGOs are known under a variety of names such as voluntary organizations, voluntary associations, voluntary agencies, action groups and private agencies. Voluntary organizations and welfare NGOs are used as interchangeable terms. Many social scientists, researchers and NGO promoters argue that there is a clear-cut distinction between voluntary organizations and welfare NGOs. For instance, in voluntary organization voluntarism exists and registration is not indispensable, but professionalism is manifested in welfare NGOs and registration is mandatory for them. Voluntary efforts stand for services independent of state. A voluntary organization is a conglomeration of volunteers joined together with shared values of concern for a specific goal.[2]

Non-governmental organizations and voluntary action groups have been part of the historical legacy. In the 19th and early 20th centuries, several voluntary efforts were started in the fields of education, health etc. The NGOs became prominent after independence, especially after 1970s. This was partly because of the limited success of past-development policies pursued by the government. Even after half-a-century of development efforts initiated by the state, the problems of poverty, hunger, malnutrition, unemployment, gender inequality, illiteracy etc., continue to plague Indian society. One of the important contributing factors for the limited success of development programmes was the absence of involvement of the people for whom the programmes were meant.[3]

There is a lot of diversity in the NGOs in India. They differ in terms of size, membership, structure, funding, and relationship with the political parties and the state, philosophy, goals and programmes. It is estimated that there are as many as 30,000 NGOs out of which about 14,000 are registered under the Foreign Contribution Regulative Act which often becomes their strength and sometimes limitation when the funds are not properly utilized.[4]

In India, especially from the Seventh Five-Year Plan, during the mid-1980s, the government not only accepted the NGOs' role in social change, but also provided them a substantial funding or economic support to the tune of about Rs 150–200 crore.

Development practitioners, government officials and foreign donors consider that non-governmental organizations by virtue of being small-scale, flexible, innovative and participatory are more successful in reaching the poor and in poverty alleviation. This consideration has resulted in the rapid growth of NGOs involved in initiating and implementing rural development programmes.

The innovative and participatory approaches adopted by NGOs are:

1. *More Action-Oriented:* NGOs are able to undertake need-based activities because they undertake studies relating to situation and needs of the people. Most of the NGOs focus on the important problems that the poor and the marginalized community such as women, dalits and adivasis face in the locality.
2. *Flexible in Methods and Practices:* NGOs exhibit a high degree of flexibility in their functioning, methods and practices as they tend to be local and small.
3. *More Focused in Development Work:* NGOs development tends to be more focused as it is their principal goal. The 'goal confusion' is one of the important contributing factors for the limited success of the government initiated programmes in India.
4. *Relative Independence:* As their governing boards are autonomous and their development activities are primarily meant for

the target groups, the methods and practises adopted in foundation and implementation of NGO development programmes, selection of the target groups, provision of services etc., are relatively independent of the local power structures.

Role of NGOs in Developmental Activities

NGOs are expected to play a vital role in all conceivable aspects of development. People as well as policymakers alike attribute innumerable roles to NGOs and presume that NGO activity is a remedy to problems in the society. Before independence, NGOs confined their role to charity, relief and welfare activities. By the second half of the 1970s, the complexion of NGOs got changed. In fact the role of NGOs itself is changing over the years due to change in the function and philosophy of other development organizations. The role of the government has changed from a police state to a welfare state and subsequently to a development state. Correspondingly, NGOs have undergone various modifications such as changes in roles as welfare development and empowerment.

The most important role of NGOs is to deliver basic services to the underprivileged people. NGOs can acquire land, construct housing for the poor, provide infrastructure such as drinking wells/pumps, food, clothing, public toilets, medical package and collection of garbage services.

NGOs also facilitate information to the government about the problems, difficulties, constraints, potentialities and aspirations of the people.

NGOs act as a catalyst for social transformation. They can also act as catalysts by encouraging different government departments to become involved with burning issues.

In this paper review of the works of the NGOs in alignment with self-help groups (SHG) is done in order to assess the empowerment of women, its extent and lacunae if any. By and large an attempt to analyze the fast track to women's development through the interface of the NGOs and self-help group programmes are examined.

Position of the Women in Our Rural Society

Women are a vital part of Indian economy, constituting one-third of the national labour force and a major contributor to the survival of the family. It is an established fact that the poorer the family, the greater its independence on women's income. Gender analysis of most social and economic data reveals that women in India continue to be relatively disadvantaged in matters of health, nutrition, literacy and productivity.

In rural India, more than 90 per cent of women are unskilled, thus confined to low paid occupations. Since they do not have control over land and other productive assets they are deprived of institutional credit. This deprivation is one of the biggest hurdles in their empowerment. Majority of agricultural labourers are women but they are mainly assigned manual labour while men perform operations involving machinery and animals.

Although the government recognizes, though lately, the need for empowerment of women and has taken several effective steps in this direction, the lot of Indian women especially in the rural areas continue to remain marginalized. The Panchayati Raj Institutions too have not been able to involve women in activities related to sustainable development. For this purpose, NGO sector alone is best suited as an agency of change. By and large, the track records of well organized and established NGOs speak of their better efficiency than the government machinery in motivating target groups, easier rapport with closer proximity to people, devotion to assigned goals and more cost effectiveness in their operations. There are many NGOs already operating in the field of gender related economic development.[5]

Women and Self-Help Groups (SHG)

Self-help groups are voluntary, small group structures for mutual aid and the accomplishment of a special purpose. They are usually formed by peers who have come together for mutual assistance in satisfying a common need, overcoming a common handicap or life-disrupting problem, and bringing about desired social and/or personal change. The initiators and members of such groups perceive that their needs are not, or cannot be, met by or through existing social institutions. Self-help groups emphasize face-to-face social interactions and the assumption of personal responsibility by members. They often provide material assistance, as well as emotional support, they are frequently cause-oriented, and promulgate an ideology or values through which members may attain an enhanced sense of personal identity.[6]

Self-help groups of women in India have been identified as an effective strategy for the empowerment of women in rural area as well as women in urban areas; bringing women together from all spheres of life to fight for their rights or a cause. Women through these SHGs work on a range of issues such as health, nutrition, agriculture, forestry, social awareness etc., besides income generation activities and seeking micro credit.

Self-help groups are emerging as major agents of development and empowerment of weaker sections in the Third World. In India, since the beginning of the Ninth Plan, most of the development programmes are channelled through SHGs. In all the parts of the country, self-help groups are organized by governmental, banks and non-governmental organizations facilitate them by providing revolving fund, organizational base and training, credit etc. It is worthwhile to call SHGs a mass movement on a national scale for development and empowerment of the poor and downtrodden in the country.

Micro-Financing in India

Credit is one of the most crucial inputs in rural development. Access to institutional credit for the rural poor is a very important precondition to any poverty alleviation strategy. Rural credit system experienced huge overdues due to repayment problem. Chronic overdues and poor recovery only hamper the development banking.

Microfinance is considered now as a powerful instrument for poverty alleviation and rural development. It is an effective intervention that is capable of reaching the otherwise unreached, by targeting and internalizing in the development process specific regions and social and economic groups. It is the supply of thrift, credit and other financial services and products of very small amounts to poor in rural, urban and semi-urban areas for raising their income levels and standard of living.[7]

In recent years, microfinance programmes have been used as not only a tool for economic upliftment but also as an effective way to meet women's practical and strategic needs.

In India, the failure of cooperatives, formal financial institutions and government subsidized programmes (such as Integrated Rural Development Programme, IRDP) to reach the targeted poor, acted as an inducement for the promotion of microfinance programme in spite of self-help groups as a viable alternative means of alleviating poverty. The first official involvement in promoting microfinance programme through SHGs in India has been taken by National Bank for Agriculture and Rural Development (NABARD) as early as in 1992, launching a pilot project for linking 500 SHGs with banks. Thereafter, formal financial institutions, government agencies and NGOs involved themselves to encourage SHG formation and linking these groups with banks. In recent times, microfinance programme through SHGs is operating across the country, albeit with multiple characteristics and performance magnitude, to reduce poverty and empower the participants.[8]

Micro-Credit Initiatives and Women Self-Help Groups

Micro-credit initiatives have become increasingly popular as a way to mobilize poor communities despite the provision of loans through specialized financial institutions.[9] Small groups are formed, and loans are allocated to members, based on group solidarity instead of formal collateral.[10] This strategy appeals both to leftists for it is based on redistribution principles, and to those on the right for it promotes self-sufficiency and independence of the poor through capitalist activities. Micro-credit schemes have been particularly targeted towards poor women, who are often discriminated against not only by institutions, but also within their own households. The provision of loans to women may then serve the dual goals of increasing household wealth and empowering females.[11]

Microfinance in India: Delivery Mechanism and Outreach

There is a wide variety of institutions in India catering with various degrees of success to the microfinance needs of the poor families.

Though banks themselves may form SHGs and after nurturing offer financial services, NGOs have a significant role in spreading microfinance among the unbanked poor. Besides their traditional activities, NGOs are effective agents in organizing, nurturing and stabilizing SHGs and ultimately facilitating their linkage with formal banking system so as to improve the outreach of the financial services to the unreached and underserved poor. The working groups on NGOs and SHGs (1995), set up by RBI, had observed that NGOs are one of the important agencies particularly suitable for empowering the rural poor and have generally been instrumental in the promotion of SHGs in different parts of the country.

In 1990s, NABARD have started an experiment with MYRADA by promoting groups, mobilizing their savings and linking them with banks for credit support. Later NABARD replicated this project all over India under the SHG-Bank Linkage Programme in 1992 and many NGOs came forward to implement this project with the cooperation of banks. In 1994, following the success of NABARD, SIDBI also came forward to provide bulk lending to NGOs in turn for lending to groups/individuals. Ministry of Human Resource Development, Government of India established Rasthriya Mahila Kosh (RMK) for providing loan to NGOs in turn to lend women.

SHGs-NGOs-Bank Linkage

SHGs formed by NGO and Linked to Bank: In this model, NGOs would organize the poor into SHGs, undertake training for awareness building, entrepreneurship and skill training, help in arranging inputs, extension and marketing, introduce saving and internal lending, help in maintenance of accounts and link them with the banks for credit requirements. Banks directly provide loans to SHG with recommendation of the NGOs. In this model, NGOs act as facilitators.

NGOs form SHGs and Perform Financial Intermediation Role as On-lender to SHGs after Sourcing Loans from Bank

In this case, besides acting as facilitators, the NGOs also work as financial intermediary. Here the loan is given to NGOs by the bank for on-lending the SHGs/individual. In this linkage model, NGOs would be legally responsible for repayment, and would bear the risk of non-payment. Involvement of NGOs in micro-credit system would have positive influence as they are grass-roots agencies with good information about borrowers thus, adverse selection and production of recovery could be avoided. At the same time, NGOs would be in a position to help rural poor, particularly women to bring them above poverty line and create rural employment.

NGOs Role in Empowerment of Rural Women

A few studies have revealed the significance of NGOs in development as they mobilize human and natural resources in rural areas. One of the salient features of the NGOs is that several socio-economic inputs are integrated for a comprehensive development. A few NGOs have been working with the labourers, destitute women and piece workers by forming self-help groups, unions and cooperatives of their own. Basically, these NGOs provide tools, raw materials and equipments to the destitute women and also cater to market their products.

They disseminate information and involve in networking between the government, donors or funding agencies, civil society and beneficiaries or target groups.

Another aspect of the NGOs is their advocacy role which is of great importance. Today, various NGOs are campaigning for participation of the beneficiaries. Participatory development also refers to the concept of empowerment of people and women in particular. NGOs have been playing their part in helping people and transforming their lives.

NGOs are building social capital in the form of groups that can generate a sound base for their members to develop their credibility as borrowers and encourage financial institutions to develop confidence in establishing lending relationships with the groups. Thus, NGOs transform the beneficiaries into 'borrowers' leading to establishment of systems and structures in which a sustainable process of linking the poor borrowers to sources of capital and other financial services with formal financial institutions is achieved.

NGOs have trained and developed the SHGs to a level where they can do business on equal terms with a bank. Social and communication barriers often make it necessary for the NGOs to introduce the group to the bank, and to foster the relationship for some time. Large number of NGOs have responded to this new 'Market', since it is a powerful method of empowering their clients and making them independent of future assistance.

Weaknesses of NGO Movement

NGOs and their development programmes also face a number of weaknesses, which are as follows:[12]

Spatial Limitation

There is the spatial dimension determined by the definition of target groups which is determined by a number of factors such as the amount of finance available, the physical characteristics of the project, the organizational size and structure of the NGO etc. Not all poor or marginalized groups will be covered within the territorial location.

Lack of Good Governance and Transparency

It has been pointed out that the large, influential and well-funded NGOs may not be able to concentrate resources in regions and sectors that are most important for national development. As a result, service delivery is taking place in the already better-off regions while the poorer states are left out.

Palliative Nature of Service Provision

Most of NGOs could only facilitate the undertaking of subsistence activities and income from such activities was either equal to or less than the existing wage income. The income from the economic activities promoted by NGOs formed only a small proportion of the total income of the families of members.

Lack of Accountability

It has been found that NGO projects, while accountable to the donors are hardly accountable to the people with whom they work. A study of 16 NGOs in Karnataka concluded that there is a mismatch between objectives and activities of these NGOs and the situation and needs of the poor with whom they work, but influenced by donor's priorities and policies.

Conclusion

In the Indian scenario, it is felt that NGOs may play the catalytic role of promoting SHGs and linking them with banks, pursuing financial intermediation on the lines of other developing countries. NGOs can be expected to fast internalize the culture and practise associated with efficient conduct of the business of microfinance. The rise of NGOs doing business in microfinance, no doubt, has opened the flood gates of aid in at least selected regional pockets in India, enabling them to completely bypass the patronage of the officialdom.

The NGOs sector is increasingly pursuing the financial intermediation as one of the effective tools in meeting their social agenda. In this context, the governments, both at the centre and states have an equally important role to play in creating conducive policy environment for the growth of this NGO sector as future microfinance institutions. Here, what is required is suitable policy framework, innovative package of services with timely credit.

NGOs have now attained legitimacy and credibility largely due to liberalization policies. But, the cooperation with the government has to take place in the very same environment which has some of the policies that go against the poor. Hence, there is need for NGOs to play a dual role, collaborate with the government critically and oppose policies of the government which are anti-poor. NGOs and their people's organizations can play this dual role only when they succeed in self-help promotion. This includes the formation of target group organizations, building capacity of the poor and leadership among them.

Many NGOs are welfare-oriented. They do not want to become involved in banking transactions, even as facilitators but prefer to remain in their traditional fields of health, education and community development. Developing countries like India need voluntary organizations for the upliftment of society. As the country is steeped in poverty and illiteracy the governmental efforts are complemented by the efforts of voluntary organizations.

Notes

1. Shamshad Ahmad, "NGOs and the Development of Rural Entrepreneurship", *Kurukshetra*, March 2005, p. 27.
2. M. Gurulingaiah, "Role of NGO in Empowerment of Tribal Women in Karnataka", *Kurukshetra,* December 2002, p. 30.
3. Laxmi R. Kulshrestha and Archana Gupta, "NGOs in Micro-financing Partners in Rural Development", *Kurukshetra,* February 2002, p. 26.

4. S.N. Pawar, J.B. Ambekar and D. Shrikant (eds.), *NGOs and Development: The Indian Scenario*, Rawat Publications, Jaipur, 2004, p. 14.
5. Syed Noman Ahmad, "NGOs and Gender Development", *Yojana*, September 2005, p. 73.
6. Rajagopal, "Empowering Rural Women's Groups for Strengthening Economic Linkages: Some Indian Experiments", *Development in Practice* (9), 1999, p. 327.
7. Tara S. Nair, "Institutionalizing Micro-finance in India: An Overview of Strategic Issues", *Economic and Political Weekly,* January 27, 2001.
8. K.G. Karmakar, *Rural Credit and Self-Help Groups: Microfinance Needs of Concepts in India*, Sage Publications, New Delhi 2001.
9. P. Mosley and D. Hulme, "Micro-enterprise Finance: Is There a Conflict between Growth and Poverty Alleviation?", *World Development* 26(5), 1999, p. 783.
10. R. Montgomery, "Displacing or Protecting the Poor? Avoiding the Social Costs of Peer Pressures in Micro-credit Schemes", *Journal of International Development*, 8(2), 1996, p. 289.
11. R. Amin, S. Becker and A. Bayes, "NGO Promoted Micro-credit Programmes and Women's Empowerment in Rural Bangladesh: Quantitative and Qualitative Evidence", *The Journal of Developing Areas* (winter), 1998, p. 221.
12. Laxmi R. Kulshreshta and Archana Gupta, op. cit., pp. 29–30.

13 Job Loss Problem and Issue of Alternative Livelihoods

Case Study of Karimnagar Cooperative Spinning Mills

M. Bharath Bhushan and E. Revathi

Around thirty thousand employees of state enterprises were relieved of the jobs owing to industrial sickness or privatization. These units in some locations were hub of the economic activity in the region and consequently with their closure a larger section of the population in the area are adversely affected. Job loss issue is a new social problem in the context of globalization and privatization and needs to be acknowledged as an important area of policy concern and social mobilization. The problem is not confined to mere government enterprises but also the private sector.

The status of post-job loss livelihoods, especially in weak economies like the Antargaon situation, is important to understand how the life world is redefined by the social status of the affected sections. Many have been relocated with the repatriates going to Tamil Nadu and some members of their family still living in Antargaon expecting payment of arrears and reopening of the unit. There is severe immiserization and casualization towards downward mobility including occupational shift towards farm employment. Local workers have attempted to find livelihoods in wage labour, farming, caste occupations and petty trade. Incomes have drastically fallen down compared to their earlier earnings.

Job loss is both economic and social problem. Some of the public enterprises have social obligations besides economic functions. The issues of job loss as an emerging social problem is examined in the context of Andhra Pradesh and a detailed assessment of the complexity is presented based on the case study. After a decade the government had paid job severance compensation and offered vocational training measures to the affected workers still living in Antargaon and surrounding area. Capacity building and job loss trauma mitigation measures need to be local and cultural specific in order to be effective. The paper also examines the pattern of changing livelihoods owing to closure of an enterprise and draws conclusions for strengthening the community effort in addressing the new social problem.

Context of Job Loss Problem

Job loss issue is an emerging social problem with significant labour adjustments in the private and public enterprises and also due to strategies emphasizing growth without employment. Job losses have a multiple implications besides loss of earnings and trauma of the affected individuals.

The problem of job losses is serious indeed. It is highly traumatic. It is considered next to the degree of suffering and trauma one faces with the loss of spouse. It has many features of the vulnerabilities and risks that are characteristic of involuntary resettlement, which are fairly acknowledged by the world community. Job loss has five of the 'eight main risks' Michael Cernea (1996) refers to in involuntary resettlement viz., joblessness, marginalization, increased morbidity and mortality, food insecurity and social disorganization while the remaining three risks also seen in some cases (landlessness, homelessness, and loss of access to common property). Job loss vulnerability has additional risks, which need to be explored further as in most cases it invariably leads to physical relocation and carrying the consequent eight main risks.

Besides social and psychological dimension the problem is of 'social problem' for sheer numbers. About 2.20 lakh workers have been laid off between 1992–93 and 2001–02 in central PSUs alone. That it continued after that also needs no mention. Amount spent on VRS for 2.20 lakh workers was Rs 6625 crore. The issue of job losses is also in vogue in state PSUs. It is on very high scale in the private sector with closures, mergers and takeovers. Magnitude of the issue as a new social problem may be appreciated by the data provided in the Table 1. The table provides details of the number of workers relieved under voluntary retirement scheme in central public sector units:

Table 1
Workers Relieved Under VRS in CPSUs

Year	*No. of workers*	*Rs in crores*
1992–93	39,816	566.72
1993–94	34,270	478.06
1994–95	15,112	250.81
1995–96	12,440	209.81
1996–97	6,593	188.00
1997–98	9,108	326.67
1998–99	1,170	97.55
1999–00	1,455	130.65
2000–01	45,625	2,001.00
2001–02	54,371	2,376.00
Total	2,19,960	6,625.27

The problem of job losses in government enterprises is referred by varying nomenclature. It is called VRS in most of the states. West Bengal refers to it as Early Retirement Scheme and proposes to relieve around 70,000 workers.

There are 123 state level public enterprises (SLPEs) comprising 40 corporations, 73 cooperatives and federations and

10 companies with Government of Andhra Pradesh (GoAP) shareholdings. Of which the 40 corporations have over Rs 5,242.46 crore in paid-up share capital and over Rs 1,869 crore in accumulated losses and employ approximately 3.50 lakh people. Cooperatives include 18 sugar mills and 12 spinning mills, in which the GoAP is the dominant shareholder. The cooperatives employing over 29,000 people, have over Rs 1,000 crore in paid-up capital, and accumulated losses of over Rs 250 crore. Altogether 22,670 employees have availed VRS benefits. A sum of Rs 340.74 crore has been disbursed to the VRS availed employees. On an average, Rs 1,48,370 was disbursed for each VRS availed employee in the state although there have been some who have received a maximum of Rs 12 lakh as in some SLPEs while a significant number of employees of cooperative spinning mills have received Rs 30,000 per head as a special compensation package owing to their short period of service in the enterprise.

The GoAP has initiated VRS policy in 1996, which is attractive and liberal than the provisions envisaged in Industrial Disputes Act. The VRS policy provides job severance compensation @ of 45 days pay plus DA, for each completed year of service or the monthly emoluments at the time of retirement multiplied by the balance months of service left before normal date of retirement whichever is less.

Besides monetary assistance GoAP has introduced trauma mitigation programme named as social safety net programme which provided free counselling and vocational training for alternative livelihoods. It is considered one of the pioneering programmes in the country. Around 6,300 VRS availed employees have received retraining assistance for alternative livelihoods through vocational training and 37 per cent of the retrained persons have been successfully redeployed. (Annexure 1 Status of Workers Covered by SSNP).

The situation faced by the job loss affected workers of SLPEs in comparison with the CPSU VRS workforce, is more difficult because of greater degree of vulnerability of the target group. High degree of vulnerability is due to several factors and a combination of such factors like job severance compensation being low, too aged to adapt to new demands of labour market, weak labour markets of the particular locations on the one hand and greater pressures for earning a livelihood to support oneself and the family on the other.

Poor Resilience and Weak Social Background of Job Loss Workers in Andhra Pradesh

Personal attributes like one's education, age, gender, caste and status in family also affect the opportunities for negotiating with the changed scenario and rate of success in their redeployment. Some of the VRS availed employees are thus relatively more vulnerable than their counterparts.

VRS amount received is Rs 1,47,036 on an average although some have received around Rs 10 lakh also and some are receiving a special package of Rs 30,000. A sample study of 3,327 VRS employees reveals that a large section (58%) of the workforce had monthly earnings between Rs 3,000 and Rs 6,000.Those earning less than Rs 3,000 per month constitute 16 per cent of the total workers. Most of the affected workers have drawn a monthly salary up to Rs 6,000.

Two out of every five VRS employees are illiterate or below matriculate. Illiterates and below matriculate job loss persons constitute 15 per cent and 25 per cent respectively among the total affected workforce. Those educated upto secondary school to intermediate constitute 34 per cent of the total workforce. Besides, majority of the affected workforce (71%) belong to backward castes, scheduled caste and minorities.

Women have more handicaps for redeployment. Job loss affected women have additional handicaps. It is observed that women take greater time to ground a self-employment venture and the investments for such ventures are also far less compared with the activities initiated by men (Chandrasekhar and Vanka, 2004). The average time taken to start a self-employment venture is 29 months for women while it is 15 months among men and the average investment in the activity is Rs 10,000 for women compared with Rs 1,38,000 for men among those who are redeployed through self-employment. The affected women experience loss of status and powerlessness in great measure.

Karimnagar Cooperative Spinning Mills: Case Study

This paper briefly examines the challenges posed by job loss problem with specific reference to the Antargaon spinning mills. Labour adjustment programmes are in the initial stages all over the country and in fact in the world. The body of knowledge and experiences in the area of addressing the issue of job losses in enterprise reform programmes is a very new portfolio for scholars as well as development practitioners and policy makers. Vulnerability of the job loss workforce of SLPEs is discussed here to explain the patterns and a detailed examination is attempted by case study of Karimnagar Cooperative Spinning Mills.

Antargaon wears a deserted look where a cooperative spinning mill and textile production centre together employing about seven hundred workers was the hub of life in the backyard of Ramagundam NTPC until late eighties. Two decades of struggle and hope to make the cooperative spinning mill was finally given up. The units became defunct and the repatriates who came to work here from Sri Lanka and Burma fled to distant lands in search of work, bread and primordial ethnic bonds. The mill was considered the ray of hope for people in the region. Antargaon spinning mills is situated a few minutes walk from their hearths and fields to the miner's jobs at Singareni Collieries. Antargaon was considered one of the areas for location of a missile range, which finally went to Chandipur in Orissa.

Other units started along with Karimnagar Cooperative Spinning Mills include Nellore Cooperative Spinning Mills and Rajahmundry Cooperative Spinning Mills where the goal was rehabilitation of repatriates. Karimnagar unit was established on 7 July, 1971 at Antargaon about 12 km distance from Ramagundam. It had a production capacity of 12,096 spindles with project cost of Rs 17.57 million. By November 1991, its net worth came down to Rs 10.3 million. It was closed on 1 November, 1991 with accumulated losses of Rs 26.88 million and arrears of Rs 14.06 million to the cotton suppliers. VRS claims have been settled in February 2000 for 398 workers with 1991 as the cut-off date consisting of permanent (258), badili (108) workers and 32 administrative and support staff. Repatriates belonging to spinning mill and the textiles unit reside in the textile colony built exclusively for the repatriates.

There is another state level public sector unit located in Antargaon called Textile Cooperative Production and Sales Society Limited. The textile unit established in 1971 also had Burmese repatriates and was under the department of handlooms and textiles. Same official was the managing director of both Karimnagar Spinning Mills and the textiles unit for some time. Textiles unit with about 300 employees was closed in 1984. These workers are neither relieved under Industrial Disputes Act nor given VRS.

Karimnagar Spinning Mills failed to take off very soon since its inception. Much before of the final closure in 1991 it was handed over to a private group named A P Yarn Combines Pvt Ltd. Private unit did not run it beyond four months. Reasons for the failure of spinning mill are many. Primarily its installed capacity had to be increased to make it profitable. It did not receive any financial assistance whereas several other spinning mills got. While other spinning mills of similar age in Andhra Pradesh were modernized three times it was modernized only once. It has no history of labour problem and its production was many times far better than other units compared to its installed capacity, claim the workers.

Post-Job Loss Changing Livelihoods: Shift Towards Informal and Farm Labour

Karimnagar Cooperative Spinning Mills had 398 workforce consisting of permanent (258), badilies (108) and 32 administrative and support staff. Of them, 36 are women. Repatriates constitute one-third of the workforce. Burmese (100) and Sri Lankan (30) repatriates were engaged in the technical and production operations. Repatriates belonging to spinning mill and the textiles unit were residing in the textile colony built exclusively for the repatriates. Now the colony is in a dilapidated state with only a few houses fit for habitation. About a decade after the closure, workers of the spinning mill received about fifty thousand rupees as job severance compensation under VRS. Most of it was used to either clear the old debts or to meet more pressing social obligations like daughter's marriage. A few also bought a piece of land in the village. Over the years, Antargaon, in the shadow of abandoned spinning mill, saw the workers shifting to cultivation or agriculture labour. A section of the repatriates have migrated to Coimbatore in search of alternative livelihoods. Only 240 out of 398 workers currently inhabit Antargaon, Goelwada and neighbouring villages.

A Profile of the Workers

Most of the VRS employees are parents with grown up children or with two to fourteen aged children. More than one-fourth (2,719.70%) is aged above 55 years. Three out of every five (61.25%) VRS employees are in the age group of 40 to 55 years. Hence they have limited scope for taking up new vocations. While the younger section i.e., those below 40 years age (11.25%) are in the situation of going for skill training for taking up new vocations the remaining are keen on making their children competitive in the labour market so that their earnings would support the family now. Their attention is more towards ensuring secured livelihoods for their children. Table 2 provides the age scenario of the VRS workforce.

Table 2
Distribution of VRS Employees by Age

Age group of VRS workforce	*Number of workers*	*Per cent to total workers*
30–39 year old	21	11.25
40–49 year old	66	34.58
50–55 year old	51	26.67
>55 years	52	27.5
Total	190	100.00

The workforce of Antargaon spinning comprises of significant number from socially vulnerable sections. Scheduled castes and scheduled tribes together constitute more than half the workers. OBC and forward caste together constitute 40.97 per cent of the total workers. Many of them were additionally vulnerable because of they were repatriates. Following Table 3 provides the details of social composition.

Table 3
Distribution of Workers by Social Background

Social category of job loss workers	*Number of workers*	*Total workers (in per cent)*
Scheduled Caste workforce	102	53.64
Scheduled Tribe workforce	2	1.20
Other Backward Castes workforce	57	20.02
Forward Caste workforce	22	11.46
Muslim workforce	7	3.69
Total	190	100.00

Economic Status

Loss of job has resulted in loss of earning and also adversely affected their chances of alternative livelihoods as they were not relieved for years. So the workers could not leave the village, which hardly had any other non-farm livelihood opportunity. For a long time, their inability to leave the spinning mill reduced their chances of recouping financially. Their morale was also affected significantly. Then a section has left for Coimbatore and also many sought employment in casual jobs. Some who could not do that also moved into caste occupations. Most of the employees were earning around Rs 3,500 per month. Their fragile economic status has been a major handicap for taking up any trade or manufacturing activity and hence became wage labour in farm and non-farm sector that is available in the neighbourhood. Their earnings are now on an average about Rs 1,500 a month.

The job severance compensation they received is very nominal. That they received it after a decade's delay made them pay most of it towards the loans they incurred during the lean period. The job severance compensation (VRS amount) being an average of Rs 47,000, there was hardly any scope for supporting any alternative livelihoods. The VRS amounts were below Rs 30,000 for a section of workers as a special compensation package and the remaining workers were paid from Rs 30,000 to Rs 1,00,000 each according to combination of one's scale and length of service.

About half the VRS employees have sought livelihoods in self-employment by running grocery shops or vegetable vending and similar works. Around one-fourth of the workers of spinning mills eke out a living by wage labour in the farm sector with daily wages ranging between Rs 50 and 65. Employment is primarily seasonal and they also work as construction labour occasionally. The technically sound VRS employees seek part time jobs in and around Ramagundam. Around one-tenth of the VRS employees have sought alternative living in agriculture. Details of the pattern of occupational shift among the respondents are provided in Table 4.

Table 4
Occupational Mobility of Former Spinning Mill Workers: A Sample

Post VRS livelihoods	*Per cent of VRS workers*	*Remarks/incomes etc.*
Reverse Mobility—Farm Sector (52)	42.28	Cultivation/farm labour/jeetham for farm labour or cattle rearing/grazing
Casual Labour—Immiserization (50)	40.65	Amali at Ramagundam market yard, cook/ayah at NTPC hostel, domestic servant etc.
Petty Trade/Self-Employed (12)	9.76	Tea stall/vegetable vendor, bakery, milk vendor, cycle shop, auto driving, RMP practice, fertilizer shop etc.
Resuming Caste Occupations (3)	2.44	Pujari, washerman,
Skeletal Staff at Spinning Mills (6)	4.88	Jr. Asst., security guard, watch and ward on consolidated pay or daily wage
	100.00	

Possibilities of redeployment and scope of alternative livelihoods of the VRS community is closely related to the local economy and the forces affecting it. Several VRS employees are negotiating with the change as individuals and collectives. There is an association of repatriates advocating the cause of house sites for the VRS employees among other pending measures to ensure their rehabilitation. Another pending issue is the allotment of two-acre land for the repatriates. Similarly, the VRS employees of Goelwada, where more than a hundred employees reside, address their issues collectively through the Gram Panchayat. Sarpanch of the village, Sri Hanumanth Reddy, is also a VRS employee. VRS employees are making efforts in convincing the potential parties to take over the unit so that they could be employed again.

VRS employees have taken greater interest in making agriculture an important source of support as cultivators or as wage labourers as it did not require any new skills. Many of them were familiar with it. Some having aptitude for entrepreneurship and access to credit have taken up self-employment in small business and manufacture. Their earnings are adequate to support the families. Growth in the present activity and access to better vocations is expected to ensure an upward mobility for most of the VRS employees.

The shift from industrial class to farming and informal sector has been the predominant form of transformation in Antargaon. There is a section, which is attempting to venture into small business and economic mobility through occupational mobility of their children. Skill upgradation in the farm and informal sectors and acquisition of new skills within the context of surrounding economy interlinked with Thermal Power Station and Singareni Collieries of Ramagundam and Mancherial is the challenge before redeployment efforts.

It is necessary to examine the village economy of Antargaon to appreciate the importance of farm and non-farm sector influences on the alternative livelihoods of the VRS community.

Impact of Job Loss on the Community

Fall of the spinning mills and related works has led to rapid transformation of farm economy reflected in shift from food crops to cotton and mechanization. Facility of canal irrigation from SRSP in 1990, transportation services through APSTRC in 1994, farm mechanization and shift in favour of commercial crops have become the vital shifts in the transformation of the village economy from spinning mill to alternative livelihoods based on local resources. RTC buses ply five times a day enabling procurement of inputs and labour from outside villages as well as marketing of agricultural produce like vegetable and milk daily.

Majority of the VRS employees found at present in the region are located in Goelwada situated 2 km from the Antargaon spinning mill. A large section of the repatriates have left Antargaon after prolonged unemployment. More than two hundred inhabitants of the village previously worked in the spinning mill. Around a hundred families living in Antargaon worked in the spinning mill and textile unit. A closer look at Goelwada reveals the changes that took place in the lives of VRS employees as a result of loss of jobs.

Until late eighties farming was primarily characterized by paddy, pigeon pea, maize, sorghum, *til* and chilli. Consumption-oriented farming has given way to market-oriented cropping pattern soon with cotton and chilli becoming the primary crops. About a hundred lorry loads of cotton is cultivated every year in the village. There are a few large size farm households with landholdings upto 50 acre each. They hoard the yields till prices become reasonable while the smaller farmers sell in distress. Majority of the farmers are small with landholdings below three acre each. Risks of cotton farming have affected the village significantly. Nine farmers have committed suicides during the past five years owing to losses in cotton yields. Two among them, Debbeti Ramulu and Matta Satyanarayana Reddy, are VRS employees who committed suicide in 1996 and 2002 respectively. Farm crisis continued to put the households in hardships and indebtedness.

Irrigation facilities through the Sri Ram Sagar project canal have also had important bearing on the changes in the village economy and the living conditions. Canal irrigation has been responsible for ensuring food security through cultivation of paddy for household needs and allocating the remaining land for commercial crops. Around thirty families are engaged in dairying and about 150 litres of milk is supplied daily to people in Ramagundam and NTPC colony.

Mechanization of agriculture through use of tractors has begun in 2000. Yella Goud was the first farmer to get a tractor in 2000. Following year Katkuru Venkat Reddy and Ananthaiah also brought tractors. Mechanization has become necessary owing to scarcity of farm hands. Women are paid Rs 30 and men between Rs 50 and Rs 60 as wages. Around 60 labourers come from Antargaon, Peddampeta and Yellampalli villages. They come by the first bus to the village at 8 am and work till 4.30 pm. Bus fares of to and from travel amounting to Rs 6 per head are also paid by the employers. While women are engaged in cotton collection and deweeding works men are mainly engaged in application of pesticides. Farm labourers from neighbouring areas come during summer in smaller numbers. Work timings in summer are between 7 am and 1.30 noon. Living on farm wages is also not that assured for the farm returned industrial workers of Antargaon spinning mills.

Conclusions

Around a thousand families in and around Antargaon had lives inseparable from the spinning and textile units. Although the Antargaon spinning mills were closed in November 1991 the workers were paid VRS after a decade. The technically sound VRS employees seek part-time jobs in and around Ramagundam NTPC town. A section of the VRS employees have sought alternative living in agriculture. Majority of the VRS employees found at present in the region are located in Goelwada village situated 2 km from the Antargaon spinning mill.

Approach to address the trauma of job loss to after a gap of almost a decade requires a special package. It is a unique situation and highly challenging as the affected group is severely marginalized. Effective policy for preparation and job loss trauma mitigation, when job losses are inevitable and are carried out in the objective manner, are essential so as to assist the job loss workers to seek alternatives. Job loss compensation needs to be provided without any loss of time from the day of relief from the job. Vulnerabilities of social and individual factors need to be assessed and on job preparation in terms of pre-VRS counselling and vocational training is the need of the hour. Special features of vulnerability like social (women and socially deprived section) and ethnic (repatriates or tribal communities) must be specially addressed.

Alternative livelihoods either for the VRS employees or through their grown up children are influenced by the local economy and relate to both rural and industrial spheres. Individual focused retraining efforts building capacities for absorption in private sector may need to be re-examined. As majority of the VRS employees inhabit two settlements adjoining the spinning mill, there is scope for integrating with community development efforts.

VRS employees form sizeable portion of the population of these two villages. Measures to prevent immiserization and engagement of the community are required. Community development measures facilitating collective action, self-help and integration with community development programmes of the government would also benefit the VRS households. Chances of redeployment based on retraining to several VRS employees are low as they are above 50 years of age. Redeployment assistance to the VRS employees would be more effective if their children are provided with vocational training to suit changing demands of the labour market.

References

Bharath Bhushan, M. (2002), "Workers of Cooperative Spinning Mills in Need of Safety Net: In the Shadow of Abandoned Mill", (mimeograph), SSNP, Hyderabad.

Bharath Bhushan, M., Uma Mohan, C. and Akhtar, Sahajad I. (2004), "Job Loss Affected Workforce in Public Enterprises: A Case Study of Social Safety Net Programme in AP", paper presented at National Seminar on Economic Reforms and Social Processes in India, 13 and 14 April, 2004, Kakatiya University, Warangal.

Cernea, M.M. (1995), "Understanding and Preventing Impoverishment from Displacement: Reflections on the State of Knowledge", Keynote Address presented at the International Conference on Development-Induced Displacement, *Journal of Refugee Studies*, Vol. 8, 3, 1995.

Chandrasekhar, P. and Vanka, Sita (2004), "Self Employment of VRS Employees in Andhra Pradesh: An Assessment", paper presented at National Seminar on Redeployment of Rationalised Employees of CPSUs: Strategies and Options, 26–27 June, 2004, NISIET, Hyderabad.

Nagesh, Sree M. (2003), "Retraining and Redeployment of Job Loss Workers: A Few Observations", (mimeograph), SSNP, Hyderabad.

Narsimha, Reddy D. (2006), "Economic Reforms, Agrarian Crisis and Rural Distress", 4th Annual, B. Janardhan Rao Memorial Lecture, Department of Public Administration and HRM, KU Warangal, AP.

Praveen, D.S. and Bharath Bhushan, M. (2002), "Perceptions of Workers and Managers on Enterprise Reforms and Job Losses", (mimeograph), SSNP, Hyderabad.

Revathi, E. (1998), "Farmers Suicide: Missing Issues", *Economic and Political Weekly*, Vol. XXXIII, No. 17.

Shama, Sharad Char and Vanka, Sita (2004), "The Job Market for VRS Employees: A Feasibility Analysis in Andhra Pradesh", paper presented at National Seminar on Redeployment of Rationalised Employees of CPSUs: Strategies and Options, 26–27 June, 2004, NISIET, Hyderabad.

Vishnu, Vardhan V. (2002), "Retraining and Redeployment of VRS Retirees: A Case Study of Adilabad Spinning Mills", (mimeograph), SSNP, Hyderabad.

Vishnu, Vardhan V., Praveen, D.S., Rajkumar, A. and Susheela Rani, M. (2004), "Utilization of VRS Amount: A Case Study of VRS Employees in AP", (mimeograph), SSNP, Hyderabad.

Annexure 1

Status of Workers Covered by SSNP

Enterprise	*Surveyed*	*Counselled*	*Trained*	*Under training*	*Redeployed*
Adilabad Spinning Mills, Adilabad	481	444	271	10	124
Allwyn Watches Limited	1486	1234	1106	0	320
AP Agros Industries Devp. Corp.	225	192	121	2	36
AP Fisheries Corpn. Limited	145	81	44	11	0
AP Handicraft Devp. Corp.	10	10	3	0	2
AP Industrial Devp. Corp.	19	16	10	0	2
AP Irrigation Devp. Corp.	483	405	210	24	113
AP Meat & Poultry Devp. Corp.	118	113	29	0	17
AP NRI Investment Corp.	8	7	0	0	0
Adilabad Spinning Mills, Adilabad	481	444	271	10	124
AP Small Scale Industries Devp. Corp.	317	283	135	1	61
AP State Finance Corp.	9	9	5	0	0
AP Textile Devp. Corp.	47	44	28	0	11
AP Electronics Devp. Corp. Limited	28	20	9	0	6
AP Spinfed	8	7	4	0	3
FEDCON	32	30	16	0	2

Cont'd...

Cont'd...

APS Handloom Weavers Coop (APCO)	209	176	106	6	19
ASM Cooperative Sugar Factory	149	135	85	25	8
Chilakaluripet Spinning Mills	383	374	185	0	56
Chirala Spinning Mills	345	341	162	46	26
Chittoor Milk Producers Coop Union	265	243	112	38	42
Girajan Cooperative Corp. (GCC)	108	33	12	3	0
Karimnagar Coop Spinning Mill	240	199	167	0	63
LIDCAP Limited	26	21	10	0	2
Nagarjuna Cooperative Sugar Factory	229	229	165	51	106
Nandyal Spinning Mills	342	331	235	0	92
Nandyal Sugar Factory	193	88	57	0	20
Nellore Spinning Mills	595	583	349	9	147
Nizam Sugars Limited	2823	2459	1507	272	487
Parchur Coop Spinning Mills	321	318	156	45	39
Rajahmundry Coop Spinning Mills	422	389	156	0	111
Sri Hanuman Coop Sugars Limited	56	55	28	0	12
Sri Krishnadevaraya Coop Oilseeds	6	3		1	0
Sri Rajarajeshwari Coop Spinning Mills	190	178	165	0	111
The Palair Coop Sugars Limited	353	307	135	74	69
Total	10671	9357	5783	618	2107

Annexure 2

VRS Employees in A.P.S.S.N.P., Hyderabad

Post-VRS livelihoods	*No. of workers*	*% of VRS workers*	*Remarks/ incomes etc*
Reverse Mobility—Farm Sector (52)		42.28	
Cultivation	5	—	Rs 6000 to 20000 per annum
Farm labour	40	—	Rs 50 daily wage
Farm labour—annual contract/jeetham	5	—	Rs 6000 to 10000 per annum
Cattle rearing—jeetham	1	—	Rs 1500 pm
Shepherd on jeetham	1	—	Rs 3000 a year
Casual labour-immiserization (50)	—	40.65	
Amali at Ramagundam market yard	1	—	Rs 100 daily
Cook	1	—	Rs 50 daily
Ayah at NTPC Hostel	1	—	Rs 500 pm
Servant at High School Teacher	1	—	Rs 600 pm
Coolie/ wage (NTPC, furniture shops)	14	—	Rs 30 to 60 daily
Contract regular at NTPC Hostel	3	—	Rs 800 to 1500 pm
Sells bread in the village	1	—	Around Rs 2500 pm
Daily wage labour	21	—	Rs 30 to 60 wage labour

Cont'd...

Cont'd…

Mason	2	—	Rs 50 to 70 daily
Digging wells manual, wage labour	5	—	Rs 60 daily wage
Petty trade/ self-employed (12)		9.76	
Tea stall	4	—	Around Rs 100 profit a day
Vegetable vending	1	—	Rs 40 a day earning
Bakery	1	—	Rs 2000
Cycle, taxi and repair shop	1	—	Rs 3000 pm
Milk vending	1	—	Rs 3000 a month
Cool drinks shop	1	—	Rs 1500 pm
Fertilizer shop	1	—	Rs 5000 pm
RMP Practice	1	—	Rs 300 a day
Auto Driver	1	—	Rs 100 daily
Resuming Caste Occupations (3)		2.44	
Pujari	2	—	Rs 1200 a month
Washerman	1	—	Rs 500 pm
Skeletal staff at Spinning Mills (6)		4.88	
Jr. Asst. at Spinning Mills	1	—	Consolidated pay Rs 2500 pm
Security guard -Spinning Mills	3	—	Consolidated pay Rs 2500 pm
Watch & Ward Spinning Mills	2	—	Rs 70 daily wage
	123	100.00	

14 Community Driven Development in Andhra Pradesh

C.P. Nagi Reddy

Andhra Pradesh District Poverty Initiatives Project (APDPIP) has been formally launched in June 2000. The Project has been contracted to Society for Elimination of Rural Poverty (SERP) through a memorandum of understanding.

Its genesis dates back to 1994–95 to social assessments and capacity assessments of the districts in 1997–99 through South Asia Poverty Alleviation Project in Mahabubnagar, Anantapur and Kurnool. The experience of SAPAP was culminating as a unique way forward for reducing the poverty during 1995–2000. APDPIP was sanctioned in May 2000 and it was formally launched in June 2000 in 6 districts. Subsequently, the project was extended to the other 16 rural Mandals in 2002 under APRPRP.

The project design reflects lessons learned from several ongoing and completed bank-financed rural development projects in India. These have shown the importance of community participation and ownership in achieving efficiency and sustainability.

They have also demonstrated how communities can contribute towards investment and operational costs if they are assured of good service. The UP Sodic Lands Project has shown how the poor can establish their own organizations and engage in multiple activities in order to mitigate risks and participate more fully in the development process. Similarly, the Integrated Watershed Development Projects, the Karnataka and UP Rural Water Supply and Sanitation Projects and the AP Forestry Project have all demonstrated the viability of user groups and their potential to manage project activities as well as to mobilize community contributions. These projects have also demonstrated the potential value of successful partnerships between community organizations, NGOs and the government.

At the operational level the main lessons incorporated into the project design are: (a) creation of a decentralized project management structure with full control over sub-project approval to expedite decisions and to minimize political interference; (b) development of streamlined procurement and disbursement rules and regulations to ensure speedy implementation; (c) inclusion of competitive employment conditions for project management staff to attract and retain competent and motivated individuals; (d) inclusion of detailed operational manuals, computerized MIS, standardized financial management procedures, regular and rigorous auditing, and quantitative and qualitative monitoring and evaluation; and (e) incorporation of physical and financial sustainability conditions in the sub-project eligibility criteria to ensure a continued flow of benefits.

In addition, a number of actions have been taken to enhance institutional readiness for implementation, including selection of the project mandals, staffing arrangements for the state, district and mandal units, preparation of the financial management manual, and development and testing of the computerized financial management system, finalization of the operational manual and guidelines for appraisal of demand-based sub-project proposals.

Project Objectives

The main objective of the project would be to improve opportunities for the rural poor to meet priority social and economic needs in the six poorest districts of Andhra Pradesh (AP). To achieve this, the project would:

(a) Help create self-managed grass-roots institutions;

(b) Build the capacity of established local institutions, especially the gram sabha/panchayats and GoAP's line departments, to operate in a more inclusive manner in addressing the needs of the poor;

(c) Support investment in sub-projects proposed by grass-roots institutions of the poor to accelerate their entry and expand their involvement in social and economic activities; and

(d) Improve access to education for girls to reduce the incidence of child labour among the poor.

Key Components: There are four key components in the project:

1. Institutional and Human Capacity Building
2. Community Investment Fund (GIF)
3. Educational Support for Girl Child Labourers and School Dropouts
4. Project Management, Monitoring and Evaluation and Studies

The Society for Elimination of Rural Poverty is implementing Indira Kranthi Patham (IKP) project. This is a statewide, community demand driven rural poverty alleviation project aiming to cover all rural poor households in the state, with a special focus on 30 lakh poorer households.

Project Scope

The project focuses on rural poor families in 914 backward mandals in 22 districts of the state. The IKP comprises of 2 projects—Andhra Pradesh District Poverty Initiatives Project

(APDPIP) and Andhra Pradesh Rural Poverty Reduction Project (APRPRP). Both are externally aided projects, with financial support from the World Bank.

The APDPIP covering 316 mandals in 6 districts with an outlay of Rs 654 crore was launched on 14th June, 2000. The project duration is upto December, 2006 and is expected to cover 9.3 lakh poor households. The APRPRP project that commenced on 1st June, 2002 with an outlay of Rs 1,486 crore covers 598 backward mandals in 16 districts of the state and is estimated to cover 20 lakh families. It also covers 260 coastal fishermen villages in non-project mandals. The project duration is from April 2003 to September 2008.

Project Implementation

The project implementation agency is the Society for Elimination of Rural Poverty, an independent autonomous society registered under Public Societies Act. The General Body consists of 25 members of whom 5 are ex-officio members and 20 non-official members. The Chief Minister is the Chairman of the General Body. Non-official members are from amongst public persons, representatives of NGOs, activists, and participating communities.

The management of the society is vested in seven member Executive Council. The Hon'ble Minister for Rural Development is the Vice President of the society and the President of the council. The ex-officio members are Principal Secretary (Department of Rural Development), Commissioner (Rural Development), Commissioner (Tribal Welfare) and Chief Executive Officer (CEO) of the society.

At the state level, there is a State Project Management Unit, consisting of CEO assisted by Regional Project Directors and other functional specialists in institution-building, training, gender, microfinance, communications, livelihoods promotion, marketing, monitoring and learning. At the district level, there is a District

Project Management Unit, headed by a Project Director, assisted by functional specialists. Through a recent government order, the P.O., IKP is also the P.D, DRDA. Specialists at both SPMU and DPMUs are drawn from government, NGOs, and open market.

At the grass-roots level, the community-based organizations—Mandal Samakhyas and village organizations—implement the various project components. The village organization is registered as a cooperative society under the Mutually Aided Cooperative Societies Act and the Mandal Samakhya is registered as a federation of cooperatives.

Target Group for IKP Project

All households below the poverty line, starting from the poorest of the poor, irrespective of caste, creed and religion, are the target group. A statewide exercise was undertaken for the identification of the poor in an open, transparent and participatory manner in the gram sabhas. The participatory identification took into account both economic and social vulnerabilities of the people. The gram panchayats have approved the lists of BPL families.

Progress of IKP upto March 2006

Institutional and Human Capacity Building

The institution and human capacity building component relates to activities that facilitate the formation and strengthening of self-managed institutions of the poor and build social and human capital. Through concerted efforts on social mobilization, out of 75.59 lakh poor households that are identified through PIP process, 54.78 (73%) poor households were brought into SHG's fold. As on today, there are a total of 6,28,507 SHGs with membership of 79,77,241 women. Almost 27,748 village organizations (VOs) and 910 Mandal Samakhyas are formed in the project districts. District Samakhyas (DS) have come into existence in all 6 APDPIP districts and in 8 APRPRP districts.

Microfinance and SHG-Bank Linkages

The SHG-Bank Linkage Programme has taken firm roots in the state of Andhra Pradesh. Nearly 25 commercial banks, 16 regional rural banks, 12 district central cooperative banks and 3,850 branches are participating in the programme. Bank lending has dramatically increased from Rs 143 crore to 85,000 groups in 2001 to Rs 2002 crore to 2,88,711 groups in 2006. Andhra Pradesh leads in SHG-Bank Linkage Programme with 40 per cent of all bank loans given to SHGs in India. The progress upto March 2006 is given below:

Community Investment Fund (GIF)

The GIF provides resources to the poor communities for use as means to improve their livelihoods. This component supports the communities in prioritizing livelihood needs by investments in sub-projects proposed and implemented by the community (SHGs/VOs/Mandal Samakhyas and other common interest groups). There are three types of sub-projects namely: (a) Income generation, (b) Productive physical infrastructure and (c) Social development. The bulk of the CIF budget is for income generation. Out of the total IKP project budget, GIF is the most important component that determines the level of employment generation for the poor. The GIF expenditure upto March 2006 is Rs 292.39 crore in DPIP and Rs 335.80 crore in RPRP working out to a total of Rs 628.19 crore. The total number of GIF beneficiaries is 18,38,686.

Land Purchase

Under this component, productive and ready-to-use land with assured irrigation facility is being given to the poorest of the poor households in the rural areas. An extent of 2,197.41 acre of land was purchased and handed over to 2,404 poor families.

Collective Marketing

The marketing interventions in IKP have registered a significant increase in this financial year. Project interventions in commodities such as lac, gum, pongaemia, shatavari and other medicinal plants have picked up in 2004–05. In addition, the VOs and MSs have successfully implemented village level collective marketing of neem, red gram, soyabean, castor, groundnut, turmeric, cashew, etc. Collective marketing activities are being undertaken in 520 mandals and 2,684 villages. The number of commodities covered is 81 with the total beneficiaries at 4,72,718.

Marketing of maize is one of the very latest marketing initiative of our project undertaken in 7 districts of Telengana where maize is grown predominantly. The objective of this intervention is to give fair terms of trade to the poor in marketing maize. Andhra Pradesh marked in association with SERP have initiated maize procurement through VOs in seven districts where maize production is predominant. Minimum support price is Rs 5,400 per metre as fixed by the Government of India. VOs set up procurement centres with all infrastructures like weights and measures, moisture-meters etc.

In Kharif, 21.88 lakh tones of maize was procured with a total value of Rs 118.18 crore. Maize procurement is in progress in Rabi season also.

Food Security

In the lean agricultural season, man of the rural poor have barely one square meal a day. The Rice Credit Line intervention addresses this hunger gap in rural communities. The scheme begins by the VOs estimating and drawing the SHG's requirement of rice from the public distribution system and distributing rice to all the families. This is repaid in weekly instalments, thus enabling food security to the members. VOs in many districts negotiate and buy better quality rice from the open system and sell it to their members at a price less than the retail outlets. The amount is also repaid in instalments. The estimated number of families benefited from food security is 9,84,393. It is estimated that it will cover 30 lakh families under food security scheme by March 2007.

Employment Generation

IKP has forged a partnership with a corporate foundation, Livelihood Advancement Business School (LABS) of Reddy's Foundation for improving their employability skills and linking the youth to service sector jobs. Vulnerable youth like girl widows, single mothers, children of landless labourers are identified by Mandal Samakhyas. They are trained for three months in life skills, personality, English language and specialized market linked skills like customer relation management (CRM), IT enabled services. These boys and girls from poorest of the poor (PoP) families are then linked to deluxe hotels, upmarket malls like Kakatiya Sheraton, Standard Chartered Bank and rural BPOs. This intervention not only helps the family economically. The number of jobs created under this initiation is 7,000 in 2004–05 and 15,300 in 2005–06.

Gender

Under this component, 36 mandal level family counseling centres were established. Many cases of violence against women were identified by social action groups. Women suffering due to alcohol abuse by husbands are being counselled by SHGs and VO level social action committees. Alternative livelihoods are identified for vulnerable groups such as Basivinis, Yanadi and Chenchu. Nearly 20,000 women are actively mobilized to stand up for their rights and to help each other. Women's understanding of justice has changed radically. Livelihoods enhanced.

Disability

The objective of this component is to help disabled persons and their caregivers to improve their livelihoods, opportunities and quality of life. The activities are carried out in 75 mandals. However, activities are also undertaken in the other programme mandals.

A total of 1,51,786 disabled persons (DAPs) have been mobilized into 15,774 SHGs, formed exclusively for DAPs. These SHGs are being federated into village organizations. Around 189 Mandala Vikalangula Sangams are formed in the state. Nearly 2,516 SHGs have been sanctioned a GIF amount of Rs 963.61 lakh. IKP has organized 406 medical camps in convergence with Disability Welfare Department and a total of 1,27,844 certificates were issued. All these certificates were issued to the DAPs with no cost to them. Almost 5,116 DAPs were covered with surgical corrections and 22,773 DAPs were provided with assistive devices, again, at no cost to them.

Health and Nutrition

This component focuses on improving the health and nutrition status of poor. It operates in a convergent mode with the line departments by looking at gaps in the existing public health and nutrition services that are provided by the line departments. It is being implemented in 44 mandals of the state. In this component, the CBOs interact with the line departments to solve their problems. In addition, they will access CIF fund for the project under the social development component. The project goal is to improve health and nutrition status of poor though empowering the communities and creating an enabling environment in 44 HN project mandals of Andhra Pradesh. About 16 nutrition centres were started to feed pregnant women. Almost 116 childcare centres were started which enabled the women to go to work and girls to schools.

Overall Performance of IKP

The overall performance of IKP is given in the following table:

Overall Performance of IKP as on March 2006

S.No.	*Indicator*	*DPIP*	*RPRP*	*Total*
1.	Total no. of SHGs under the project	1,59,925	4,68,582	6,28,507
2.	No. of DAP SHGs (included in the above total)	4,650	11,124	15,774
3.	Total no. of members in all SHGs	22,12,631	57,64,610	79,77,241
4.	Total no. of DAPs in SHGs (included in the above total)	59,985	91,801	1,51,786
5.	No. of village organizations formed	9,807	17,941	27,748
6.	No. of Mandal Samakhyas formed	316	594	910
7.	No. of MRPs/CRPs/CFs/CAs/Book keepers working	40,554	45,124	85,678
8.	No. of paraprofessionals working	3,654	2,802	6,456
9.	Total no. of beneficiaries of IGA SP sanctioned	8,91,922	9,46,764	18,38,686
10.	No. of households benefiting from food security	3,54,331	6,36,411	9,90,742
11.	No. of SHGs linked to banks (This Year)	81,594	2,57,541	2,28,711
12.	Amount of bank linkage (Rs crore) (This Year)	525.81	1,464.16	2,001.84

Best Practises of IKP

To sum up, the best practises of the Indira Kranthi Patham can be summarized as follows:

Targeting of Poor

The identification of the poorest of the poor and the poor families has been done by the village community themselves through a participatory approach. This statewide participatory exercise of enumerating 1.34 crore households in the rural areas and classifying each family as ultra-poor, poor, above poverty line and non-poor on the basis of indicators selected by the community is first of its kind in the country. The poverty document is being utilized for targeting anti-poverty measures.

Women Self-Help Movement

Universal Coverage: The women's movement in AP is the largest in the country and accounts for more than 40 per cent of the total self-help groups in the country. The goal is to cover all rural poor women into self-help groups. Out of 75.59 lakh poor families in the state, around 54.78 lakh (73%) had been organized into self-help groups in the rural areas by March 2006. It is expected that by March, 2007, 90 per cent of the rural poor would be organized.

Institutional Design

The process of federation of all self-help groups into village organizations and village organizations into Mandal Samakhyas and Mandal Samakhyas into Zilla Samakhyas is unique to the state of Andhra Pradesh and is one of the major achievements of the project. This institutional arrangement enables the SHGs to access financial services and public services effectively. The challenge is in ensuring that these institutions become financially and managerially self-sustaining.

Capacity Building of Institutions of Poor

The systematic training given to self-help groups, village organizations, Mandal Samakhyas and Zilla Samakhyas on such a large scale is unprecedented in the country. This is done through a large number of village level social activists and paraprofessionals and a large number of young and committed development professionals. The unique feature in the project is that all of them are accountable to the people's institutions—MSs and VOs.

Financial Access

The self-help groups in Andhra Pradesh have accessed bank loans to a tune of Rs 1,238 crore in 2004–05 and Rs 2001 crore in 2005–06. The self-help groups have demonstrated a very high repayment record (more than 95%). Andhra Pradesh accounts for 40 per cent of the total funds given to self-help groups through banks.

Community Managed Food Security

The food security initiative under Rice Credit Line covered around 9.85 lakh families by March 2006. The plan is to cover 30.0 lakh families by 2006–07.

Reaching out to Persons with Disability

The disability interventions, which have enabled more then 1.5 lakh persons with disabilities in the rural areas to be organized and develop their own livelihoods is the largest initiative.

Collective Marketing

The SHG federations have enhanced returns to their poor producer members in selling their agriculture, horticulture, forest produce and medicinal plants at the village level. This activity has been undertaken by more than 2,650 VOs in the state and has benefited more than 4.73 lakh members. They have handled 81 different commodities. Based on their marketing capabilities, the state government has entrusted the operation of minimum support price intervention at village level for maize to the VOs.

Green Initiative

The country's largest non-pesticide management in agriculture initiative is underway in the state and is being implemented by the

SHGs with support from NGOs. An area of 24,000 acre is being covered with this initiative. Based on the success this year, it is proposed to scale it up 10 times next year to cover 2.5 lakh acre.

Community Managed Health and Nutrition Interventions

In order to strengthen the capability of the poor to handle their health issues, the project has initiated interventions like health risk fund, preventive health education and community health activists, nutrition centres for pregnant and lactating mothers, medical care cover for their members by tying up with private medical college and hospital, life insurance run by Zilla Samakhya, etc.

Convergence

The convergence of all line departments with the activities of the self-help groups and their federations is very unique. The secretaries and head of departments of key departments like health, education, nutrition, disability, land administration, forest, etc., have been proactive in involving the self-help groups and their federations in the activities of their departments. The active role of the District Collectors in forging convergence between various line departments and the SHGs and their federations within the district is a very commendable system in AP.

SHGs and their Federations

The SHG is a collective of poor women belonging to the same socioeconomic group. The self-help group of women promoted in the state of Andhra Pradesh have the following distinctive features:

(a) The SHGs hold regular meetings once in a week/fortnight.
(b) The members save Rs 30–40 a month.
(c) Savings and accumulated interest are used for giving loans to the members.
(d) The SHGs maintain their own books of accounts.

15 Regional Diversities in Indian Development

Sunanda Pande

The diversities characterize the varied economy of India. The diversities are partly related to India's varied history. The diversity also relates to the make of Indian Constitution which identifies many areas of governmental action that are crucial to economic and social development as purely state subject. The historical diversities are even reflected in the legal structure of Indian union. An understanding of the Indian economy has to be understood by an adequate recognition of deep-seated regional diversities and heterogeneities.

Given the extremely heterogeneous character of the Indian society, India's economic policies have undergone much change over the last few years and more changes are in the process of being implemented. The central approach underlying these reforms initiated in 1991 involves a greater reliance on the market mechanism and this translates into a class of public policies including deregulation and reduction of governmental controls greater autonomy of private investment, less use of the public sector, more opening of the economy to international trade, less restrictions on the convertibility of the rupee etc., while many critics had wanted faster reforms there can be little doubt about the gathering force and grouping reach of the reforms or about the break that has been initiated in the established conventions of Indian planning and policy making. No such thing happened in Indian economy during pre- or post-independence period.

Outside India the reforms have been fairly universally welcomed but they have been since their inception, the subject of severe debate within India. The controversies have been extensive and the arguments on each side quite forceful and firm.

There are two elementary points of departure. First there must be an attempt to link the strategies of development to something more fundamental in particular, the ends of economic and social development.

Why do we seek development? What can it achieve, if fruitful? How are the successes and failures of policies including the 'reforms' of traditional policies to be judged? It is only with an explicit recognition of the basic ends that debates on means and strategies can be adequately founded.

The second basic departure takes us beyond the scrutiny of ends to the investigation of means. What are the means that have to be employed to achieve these ends? While the debates on the current reforms concentrate on a particular class of means related to use or non-use of markets such as incentives for private investment, reliance on international trade etc.

There are other means especially dealing with the social side of economic operations and success. Achievements of even the limited objectives of the current reforms will depend on conscious and organized pursuit of the social means on which economic performance and results are frequently conditional.

The deep diversities characterize the varied economy of India. The diversities are partly related to India's varied history before and after independence. But the diversity relates also to the nature of Indian Constitution which identifies as 'state subject' many areas of governmental action that are crucial to economic and social development. The historical diversities have tended to be consolidated and reinforced by the legal structure of the Indian union. An understanding of the Indian economy requires an understanding of deep-seated regional diversities and heterogeneities.

Regional Diversities and Contrasts

Given the extremely heterogeneous character of the Indian economy and society, India's achievements and failures cannot be understood in composite terms and it is essential to examine the experiences in sufficiently disaggregative form and in adequate detail, Kerala, West Bengal and Uttar Pradesh achievements in the social fields. Kerala has been quite remarkable including an achieved life expectancy of over 72 years (69 for males and 74 for females by 1991) that compares well with China's (69 years) and South Korea's (71 years) achievements despite the much greater economic development of these other countries. At the other end, Uttar Pradesh remains one of the most backward states. This state with 140 million people is also a socially deprived state. We have to explain the reasons for the backwardness of Uttar Pradesh mixed development of West Bengal with same achievements and failures and success in Kerala. We have to identify the success and deficiencies and link them with the nature of policies pursued and overall political economy of West Bengal.

The internal diversities in India offer a great opportunity to learn from each other. Lessons from other countries can also be taken as examples. Though Kerala is successful in social fields it has to learn how to generate and stipulate straight-forward economic growth in an area in which it has been conspicuously unsuccessful.

Some lessons from abroad have been debated by economists in motivating the ongoing reforms and deregulation. Some parts of the essential lessons—related in particular to the generation of social opportunities have been particularly neglected in the typical readings of these experiences.

One of the broad conclusions that emerge is the need for much more radical change in Indian economy and society in order to achieve the basic goals that were unaccomplished. The problem with the economic reforms currently underway is not that they are not needed nor that they are overexacting but that they are basically inadequate and unbalanced? The departures are too moderate and too tolerant of parts of the established tradition of economic planning in India. More radicalism is needed at this time.

On India's 'tryst with destiny' on the eve of independence in August, 1947, Jawaharlal Nehru reminded the country that the task ahead included the ending of poverty and ignorance and inequality of opportunity. Some achievements have been made in these general areas including the elimination of famines, fairly successful functioning of our democratic system was the emergence of a very large and quite successful scientific community—achievements that compare favourably with what has happened in many parts of the world. Much of the task that Nehru had identified remains largely unaccomplished and we have fallen quite far behind the best performs. We have to examine those obstacles and see how they can be eliminated.

Economic growth is valuable because it helps to eradicate deprivation and to improve the capabilities and the quality of life of ordinary people. The first and foremost important aspect of Nehru's listing of what we have to do is to make clear the elimination of illiteracy, ill-health and other avoidable deprivations are valuable for their own sake. They are the tasks that we face. The more conventional criteria of economic success such as high growth rate, a sound balance of payments etc., are to be valued only as a means to deeper ends. It would therefore be a mistake to see the development of education, health care and other basic achievements only or primarily as expansions of 'human resources'—the accumulation of 'human capital' as if people were just the means of production and not its ultimate end. The bettering of human life does not have to be justified by showing that a person with a better life is also a better producer. Basic education, good health and other human attainments are not only directly valuable as constituent elements of our basic capabilities, these capabilities can also help in generating economic success of a more standard type which in turn can constitute to enhancing of quality human life even more. Many of the ingredients of a good quality of life including education, health and elementary freedoms clearly do have instrumental roles in making us more productive and helping us to generate more outputs and incomes. The world over the last few decades have forcefully drawn attention to the instrumental importance of education, health and other features of the quality of human life in generating fast and shared economic growth.

In looking back at what Jawaharlal Nehru saw as our 'tryst with destiny, we must assert:

1. The inalienable eminence of basic capabilities and the quality of life in judging the success of economic and social policies.
2. The contingent but significant practical importance of many of these capabilities especially those related to education, health and elementary freedoms in promoting economic growth and through it further advancing the quality of life of people.

Learning from Others' Experience and from India

India can learn a lot from the experiences of other countries, which have been better than our country. We have to even learn from our experiences. The average levels of literacy, life expectancy, infant mortality etc., in India are enormously adverse compared with China, Kerala does better than China. In adult female literacy rate, India is 39 per cent, China is 68 per cent and Kerala is 86 per cent, higher than China. In terms of rural female literacy, Kerala has a higher achievement than every individual province in China. Compared with China, Kerala has higher life expectancies at birth (69 for males and 74 for females compared with China's 68 and 71 years respectively). A lower fertility rate (1.8 and China 2.0) and much lower rate of infant mortality (17 and 16 per thousand respectively for boys and girls in 1991 compared with China's 28 and 33 years respectively).

These are great many things that we can learn from within the country by using diversity of our experiences particularly in use of public action.

While the encouragement of economic incentives and opportunities has varied between different parts of the country, there has been a generally counterproductive regulational environment in India that has restrained economic growth all over the country over many decades. In the recent reforms, the issue of learning from the experiences of more successful reforms has picked up.

Counterproductive Regulations and Necessary Reforms

Comparison of India with the experiences of other countries is often made to motivate changes in economic policy for e.g., to defend a programme of economic reforms—involving liberalization of trade deregulation of governmental restrictions, encouragement of private initiative etc. South Korea, Hong Kong, Singapore have made remarkable achievements. Other countries like Thailand, China have made use of market-based economic opportunities.

The counterproductive nature of some of the governmental restrictions, controls and regulations has not only interfaced with the efficiency of economic operations but also failed to promote any kind of real equity in distributional matters. The privileges were often exploited for the sectoral benefit of those with economic, political and bureaucratic power of those with the opportunity to influence people with such power.

There is a greater scope to integrate with the world market which is quite rewarding even for India. But there is a lurking fear of institutional controls from GATT and other international institutions.

Economic Development through Social Opportunity

The central issue in economic development is to expand the social opportunities open to the people.

The creation and use of social opportunities on a wider basis requires free markets. They call for an active public policy that could enable people to use the opportunities that the possibility of more trade—domestic and international offers. Perhaps above all it calls for a rapid expansion of basic education overcoming the massive illiteracy and educational backwardness in India. This requires the provision of literacy and elementary indication as fundamental opportunities for all and the spread of secondary education on a very much wider basis. India's record in both these aspects in quite dismal despite the fact that literacy and school education have been part of the rhetoric of Indian planning since independence.

Besides education there are also other expansions of social opportunities that call for urgent attention. These include the need for more widespread and better health care, greater access to provisions of social security, more effective land reforms and in general enabling the more constrained sections of the population to lead a less restrictive life including being more free to make use of the facilities that the spread of markets could provide.

References

The sources of these data include coal (1993), Office of the Registrar General of India 1993, World Bank (1994), UNDP (1994) and Drize and Savan.

(1995) The life expectancy estimates for India for 1991 are provisional and drawn by the author from unpublished data at the Registrar General's Office.

Contributors

M. Bharath Bhushan, Founder Secretary, Centre for Action Research and People's Development, Hyderabad.

V. Janardhan, Assistant Professor, Department of Sociology, University of Hyderabad, Hyderabad.

Thilotham R. Kolanu, Assistant Professor, Administrative Staff College of India, Hyderabad.

Jadi Musalaiah, Department of Political Science, Nizam College, Hyderabad.

B.C. Muthayya, Formerly Deputy Director General, National Institute of Rural Development (NIRD), Hyderabad.

C.P. Nagi Reddy, State Project Manager, SERP, Andhra Pradesh.

K. Padmavathi, Department of Sociology, Nizam College, Hyderabad.

Sunanda Pande, Associate Professor, Department of Sociology, Nizam College, Hyderabad.

Vinita Pandey, Department of Sociology, Nizam College, Hyderabad.

R.B. Patil, Department of Sociology, Shivaji University, Kolhapur.

Jyotsana Rajvanshi, Coordinator, NGO Centre, IDS, Jaipur.

D. Narsimha Reddy, Centre for Handloom Information and Policy Advocacy, Hyderabad.

S. Jeevananda Reddy, Formerly Chief Technical Advisor, WMO/UN and Expert-FAO, Convenor: Forum for a Sustainable Environment.

E. Revathi, Fellow, Centre for Economic and Social Studies, Hyderabad.

Praveen Sriramshetty, Project Director, Society for Participatory Research in Asia (PRIA).

Swarna S. Vepa, Programme Director and Ford Foundation Chair of Women and Sustainable Food Security at MSSRF, Chennai.